Turning Leaves

ILLUMINATING

An ^Anthology of Prose and Poetry

Dr. Audrey Lavin and Dr. Ray Gehani, Editors

Turning Leaves

ILLUMINATING

An ^Anthology of Prose and Poetry

Originated by
the Wednesday Writers Workshop

Dr. Audrey Lavin and Dr. Ray Gehani, Editors
WWW Creative Publishers

Library of Congress Catalog Card Number: 2011903340
ISBN: 0615455867
ISBN - 13: 9780615455860
Editor Lavin's Photograph by Lauren Shay Lavin
Nature Photographs by Steve Endres

WWW Creative Publishers

Dedication

Editors Audrey Lavin and Ray Gehani dedicate this anthology to their families and friends.

Thanks, everyone.

Acknowledgements

It has been a joy for us to work with the 30 North Eastern Ohio writers represented in this anthology.

This book would not have been possible without the grants and enthusiastic support of the following organizations and individuals:

The Akron Manuscript Club

The Akron Italian American Association

The Canton Poetry Society

Ray Gehani

Barbara M. Harkness

Bill Howland

Audrey Lavin

Carl H. Lavin

Stephanie Steiner

Wednesday Writers Workshop

Caroline Weldon

A word from the editors:

When we look at the falling leaves in autumn and the sprouting new leaves in spring, we are reminded of how life renews and revives itself. As change with time is a defining feature of nature and the universe, so we expect that change and renewal will be a defining feature of your readings in *Turning Leaves*.

We hope that as you turn the leaves of the poetry, creative non-fiction, fiction, and memoir that comprise this book, you will find inspiration, humor, and connection. Our contributors are men and women, young and old, native-born and immigrants.

We know that the murmur of compassion and the sound of potential laughter are sometimes hard to hear above the banging noise of our day-to-day lives. Members of the Wednesday Writers Workshop believe that time spent with literature, such as *Turning Leaves*, can sharpen ears and open eyes to new perspectives.

Enjoy.

Audrey and Ray

Table of Contents: Sections and Contributors

Section IV: Medical Memoir

Section V: Contributors

Poetry

ALL FLESH IS GRASS, AND ITS GLORY AS THE FLOWER OF THE GRASS

Bob Barrett

Wonderful temple of cedar and stone
High on Mount Zion like God's royal throne
Sneering at Babylon, for it is known
No holy city can be overthrown

>Mourn, Israel, you are bereft
>Now not one stone on another is left

Feasting with hundreds of friends in his hall
The king watched a hand write strange words on his wall
Daniel the Hebrew read out to them all
Weighed and found wanting, your kingdom will fall

>Weep, Belshazar, you shall not lead
>God gives your kingdom to Darius the Mede

Out on the plains where fat buffalo graze
Placidly passing the last of their days
Trusting in numbers, not changing their ways
Steam locomotives advance through the haze

>Graze, buffalo, under the sky
>Fearlessly feed and so suddenly die

Down the broad avenues armies parade
Missiles worth millions so proudly displayed
Trusting in technical things they have made
Burying bodies with simply a spade

>Fly, fighter jets, sail, submarines
>Die for the oil to fuel your machines

Colorful flowers of mountain and moor
Dry up and perish, although they are pure
What God has spoken is solid and sure
The word of the Lord shall forever endure

    Bloom, flowers, for your day shall pass
    All that grows withers, and all flesh is grass

ODE TO THE SANTA ANA WIND
Bob Barrett

She flirts with disaster and plays with fire
Speeding down the mountain in her red convertible, trailing dust
She overrules the weather forecast
No more smog, no chance of rain
Not to be confused with Claus, this Santa takes and takes
Tarnishing everything with ashes and soot
As she turns a blowtorch on the chaparral-covered hills
She has nothing to give except a bad time
This is one prima donna too hot for Hollywood
You'll find her in the smoking section

UNSEEN ANGELS
Bob Barrett

Angels are servants, completers of orders,
Messengers from the Almighty above
Scaling down actions to human proportions
Shifting small items that just need a shove
Watching a human sleep soundly must be for them

Some sort of spectacle, thrilling and strange
Far more exciting than ten thousand ages
Waiting in Heaven for something to change
Down here on Earth all is pure imperfection

Turbulent motion all night and all day
Everything moving in every direction
Action, reaction, and death, and decay
People in danger face greater temptations

Those most in pain seek for any way out
Here on Earth everyone needs some attention
Those firm in faith are still subject to doubt
During the times when our souls are in peril

Angels do battle around us, unseen
During the lulls between tempests and tyrants
They help the poets and artists succeed

Violent eras bequeath us great riches
Paid for in terror that pierces the heart
Out of the crucible pours finer silver
Out of great suffering blooms finer art

Where does that leave me, a man without crises
Happily married, not under much strain
Blessed with security, health, and abundance
Rarely afraid, and a stranger to pain?
Just like a sleepwalker I'm in no hurry

Like a balloon in a hurricane's eye
Blithely expecting to live to a hundred
Reasonably sure it's not my turn to die

As I sit pondering odd paradoxes
Comes to my mind a disquieting thought
What if I actually am in great peril?
What if I took one more chance than I ought?

Just like a sleepwalker I'm in no hurry
Muddling along without care, without fear
Treading a minefield alone in the moonlight
No, not alone, for the angels are near

Humans are subject to myriad dangers
Floods and tornadoes and earthquakes and drought
Down to microbial pathogens lurking
I'll live much happier not finding out

A CENTURY THROUGH CICADA EYES
Bob Barrett

A tough year for Cicadas, 1897
Sawmills expand where the forests still stand, falling fast
New Americans swarm like moths as Lady Liberty's torch draws
more
Sill cicadas sing, lay eggs, and wait for seventeen years

A better year for Cicadas, 1914
Trees increase across forty-eight states as horseless carriages belch
forth foul fumes
The last passenger pigeon dies at the Cincinnati Zoo
Four-winged craft take flight, roaring louder than cicadas ever
could

A moderate year for Cicadas, 1931
Abandoned farms start sprouting trees, fine fodder for the future
Oklahoma dust darkens skies as farmers crawl upwind to California
Nobody hears the cicadas, while sitting around the radio

A mixed year for Cicadas, 1948
More trees, thanks to the CCC, but watch out for the DDT
And atom bombs are deadlier still
A World War won and a Cold War begun, the cicadas sing

A time to die, 1965
Winter warms to silent spring as endrin and aldrin end all insect life
And songbirds drop dead in droves
Sacrifices must be made, they say, while sending soldiers to
Vietnam

A time to recover, 1982
The air clears across the Rust Belt as smokestacks gasp their last
At the Cold War's height they halt the summer heat
Shut safe inside their air-conditioned malls, nobody hears the
cicadas

A fine year for Cicadas, 1999
As the air becomes cleaner and the suburbs grow greener
The economy hums along to the cicadas' frenzied song
The present never looked better or the future brighter

God only knows, 2016
Come back to behold what the best and brightest bring us
You just never can tell, seventeen years in advance
One thing is sure, the cicadas will sing

SHIPPING OUT

Ben Bartman

The sea awaits your ship as the darkness for the light,
Your charts are lined with plans that assure your port's in sight.

With parent packed provisions free will departs the dock.
But by-gone ghosts, a misty freight, ballasts your ship like rocks

The land becomes unbounded as the ropes are tossed on board,
Your leeway widens wind-filled sails and your future seems assured.

Your will is free to sail the sea to choose your ship's next calling
Your freedom swells as wind-filled sails billow before the yawning

And secretly tended, hide on board powers beyond your ken,
That older winds with hidden strengths should not be mistaken.

But hoary gusts begin to blow when a change you plan to make.
Because the ancient breaths recall yearnings for their own sake.

The ethos of those prior lives remain enigmas in our world,
They have a legacy so tenuous they cannot be unfurled.

Their loves, hates, beliefs and feelings are forever kept alive,
In the secret lessons learned in youth, their truths still survive.

Little do you know about the passions from your past
About anger, trust and lust held fast against the mast.

About the enduring truths of life more basic than religion
Your parents passed them on to you in secrets never written

You cannot sail your will alone. Let not hubris shade your mission.
You share your sails with airy gusts that blow from ancient visions.

AN ODE TO SKIERS
Gordon Bryant

Like great musicians with instruments finely tuned,
Playing songs instrumented by Masters
In perfect harmony unfolding
With fingers deftly moving-
Flying, touching, caressing
We ride this great white wave to unseen beyonds.

Like the slippery snake,
With serpentine power glide.
Our feet with movements foreign
We slip, we slither, we slide.
This great white mass we measure
The monument we overtake and we reign.

We set sail on gravity's ocean-
Where fantasies become reality-
Where dreams become life-
Where weightless we flow
Through this sea of great peace.
The mountain congratulates-with sweet memory.

Like the eagle on the wind
New heights we reach untold
In a realm known mostly to birds-
This secret, now ours to hold.
To swoop, to soar, to scale all boundaries
And to be alone- - - but not lonely.

Yes, we tread where angels dare,
At the threshold of Heaven's door.
Where greeted by the touch of light
And beckoned by the thrill of knowing.
Where smiles like flower bloom
On faces beaming like the sun.

THEY SAY

Peggy Brunyansky

after Hurricane Katrina, New Orleans
August 2005
They always do say
the levee won't hold.
Been here nigh on 60 years,
39 with her, 40 come June.
Seemed like the wind was different
than we ever heard it,
like a train comin'
just like they tell you.
We was gatherin' up the pictures
when the water hit,
broke the house plumb in two,
knocked the photos from our hands,
took the albums too,
all of them,
begun when we was in high school together.
She wailed,
soundin' like a new-made widow,
and I reached to hold her just as the second wave come.
Right hand locked on the doorframe of our room,
I held her hand with my left, just like we always done,
in good times and bad, but life-or-death tight,
looking down at her face for what seemed hours.
Wind didn't let up, water didn't let up,
but her tears did and her light that I've loved
since I wasn't but 16 year old got brighter in her eyes.
She made her mouth into a kiss, whispered
"take care the grandbabies, honey" and
slipped away.

This here is her at our senior prom. The corners is a little mussed.
They do say the first year is the hardest.

11

NO WORDS
Peggy Brunyansky

Lake Hope, Ohio 2001
When my oldest son was small,
the neighbor came to visit every afternoon, Scrabble game in hand.
We played for hours while our babies slept,
drinking sweet tea and talking girl talk,
stretching our minds beyond motherhood,
building friendship that would last forever,
She always won.

This fall weekend,
I share a rustic cabin with my grown son.
Night sounds reach through screens—
crickets,
boats heading out for night fishing,
occasional laughter—
to tug at our senses,
sharpened with no telephone, no TV.
We discover an old Scrabble game
hidden away in the rafters and,
in the dimming light,
read rules to help failing memories.
(Has it really been 30 years since I've played Scrabble?)

I have all vowels, one point each, and can form few words.
Then I have no vowels, all consonants and again no words,
maintaining my tradition of losing.
The bank is empty, our pieces grow fewer.

We spend long moments staring at the board.
At last, my son sets down two tiles, a word–
O-X, ox, 10 points.
He is pleased.
I place a P in front of his word, pox,
Triple Word Score, 36 points.

"You suck," says my son.
A belly laugh,
stored away with his childhood,
with afternoons of sweet tea and girl talk,
fills me.
I am his age again with life stretching before me, all good.

MAY BEEEE
Peggy Alder Brunyansky

For Grandpa, Eugene Charles Alder
Partridge Lake, New Hampshire – 1954

The screen door slammed
before the day was fully lit.
Beside me, my sister's breath
lifted and dropped, lifted and dropped
a curl of her hair.
My pillow smelled of Grandma's funny brown soaps
that lived, hidden among the linens,
like shy turtles.
Johnny and Grandpa whispered their way down the needled path.
Sunken log steps were dew-slick.
Johnny held tight to the white birch tree rail.
Grandpa, 70 years of New England in his bones,
walked tall.
Boats turned their noses towards the favorite fishing spots,
voices mingling in an early morning chorus.
Grandpa's laugh,
carried back by the lake,
was young.

THE BASTARD

Marie T. Cox

Slowly, we passed through the gate–Traitor's Gate–
And the boat gently stopped.
I could not move, not at all.
My heart beat as if in my throat–
My eyes would not rise.
A hand at my elbow urged me on.
Still I sat. Numb, unbelieving.
What awaited me here?
The same fate as my mother, the "whore" of England Past?
Finally, I rose, unsteadily at first.
My eyes flickered toward the steps.
Up, up, up…
Slowly up the stairs, the stairs of the damned.
Courage, Elizabeth.
The night was cold, and a mist rolled in over the cobblestones.
A chill ran through my bones as we approached the Bloody Tower.
The soldiers' torches cast frightening shadows.
How many had my father sent there, to that tower?
Through the mist, another structure loomed larger and larger–
My legs almost faltered. Not for me, the daughter of a king!
Softly, a voice came from the shadows, "Come, my lady. This way."
I could see it clearly now…the wooden scaffold.
It waited, oh so patiently, for its next victim.
Mother, will I see you soon?
I, Elizabeth?

MICHAEL DELL STORY

Lindsey Figiel, MBA Student

Dell broke from academia's cell,
To become a transformational leader that all would know well,
He speaks with authority but listens to those below,
As though they have something different to bestow.

Born into a family of physicians,
He didn't follow their wishes.
He left his studies in biology,
He created a company in the new age of technology.

His company excels at just-in-time delivery,
Employees are rewarded monetarily if business goes merrily.
He negotiates and collaborates with all those he meets,
As if there is a different perspective yet to be seen.

He puts his name on everything he creates,
And dares to be different from those he faces.
He has powered his company into the next generation,
By focusing on delighting customer relations.

To innovate and grow like never before,
To stay ahead of the game with new inventions and more.
To be productive he manufactures in large numbers,
With a little added room for people's preferences.

He is quick to deliver, so not to wither,
To achieve what no other hi-tech company can tether.
Fancying to be in the top three,
He only wants the most talented people on his team.

He may not be liked by everyone, including his staff,
But he waves it off every chance he is able to catch.
What matters to him most is finding stability,
In order to spend more time with his family.

To take a chance to change the world,
He still values trust and integrity the most.
His company tries to protect their surroundings,
By reducing, reusing, and recycling.

He gives back to those in need,
By doling out millions for catastrophes,
Wanting a more promising future for all those involved,
His claim to fame is to strive for a better tomorrow.

INTERROGATIONS
Daniel Gallik

Uncle Joe told me at least one phone
in the house ought to be a dialer.
I never questioned Uncle Joe.

I never asked my wife why she ate
only Kellogg's All Bran. I never
asked any of my four daughters

if they had a period recently. One
day I went over to Jones Hardware
to see if they had windshield

washer fluid. And they did. And I
felt good about that. And bought
2 gallons right there.   The other

day I asked my doctor whether I
had cancer. He did not have a smile
on his face when he told me.

NEVER MAKING AN ERROR
Daniel Gallik

She always sat in the back of the room.
Of course, everybody tries to do that.
But she always succeeded. Her teachers
never asked her any questions. Yes, she
would slide by in every class. Get A's

in gym. She got to college, did the same
thing. Her major. elementary education.
She ended up teaching in the inner city.
She did okay. The kids did okay. Hubby
was happy. They had two kids. Kids did

okay. After 30 yrs. she retired. Got a job
selling women's clothes at Dillard's.
Did fine there. Worked thirty years
there. Retired at the age of eighty two.
Worked 30 hours a week at her church.

Just died ten minutes ago in her sleep.
Her hubby had passed 10 yrs. ago. He
was happy. They lived well. Kids got
a load of money. The two were
the only ones who remembered her.

MY POEM, HUNTRESS
Ray Gehani

Sometimes my poem
Leaps at me
Like a lion
Hiding in bushy shadows of my heart.

Sometimes my poem
Teases me
Like a tiger
With a tail tucked between legs.

Sometimes my poem
Flies freely
Like an eagle
Going here, there, and everywhere.

But sometimes my poem
Sings to me
Like a cuckoo bird
From the core of my soul.

TO A PREACHER
Ray Gehani

Share what you have earned
Teach what you have learned
Transform in others
Only what you liberated in you.

You are one with the cosmic spirit
Stay true to your authentic core
Connect with others
Just other parts of your cosmic parts.

What matters most is to love
Love self first and then others.
Be compassionate in your giving
And passionate in living in the moment.

You evolved to become the teacher
Do not regurgitate your inheritance
Stand on the firm foundation of
Your own learning, living, and loving.

I MISS MY DAD
Ray Gehani

I miss my dad who died on railway tracks,
He always tried to tell me what not to do.
When to wake up, and where to go.
I wish I had agreed with him more.

I miss my dad who died on railway tracks.
He practiced more, and preached much less,
Living a life of principles and integrity.
I wish I had admired him more.

I miss my dad who died on railway tracks.
He loved and collected books,
He read wide and deep, and shared what he read.
I wish I had read with him more.

I miss my dad who died on railway tracks.
He brought home unexpected gifts,
And he took me to inspiring films.
I wish I had thanked him more.

I miss my dad who died on railway tracks.
He encouraged, urged, and inspired me to fly high,
He came to my awards, and celebrated my joys.
I wish I had said Thank You to him more.

YOUR PERFECT STORM

Ray Gehani

Your heart ebbs hopelessly without sail,
In a frothy sea of emotions.
Not knowing when the next tide would come,
I will take you back to your shore.

Your mind hurts,
Unable to share or split
The deep sorrows of your friend gone.
I am available to guide you back home.

Your body aches,
Too weak to support
Your scaffoldings corroded by grief.
Just hang on to me, to rebuild your strength back.

Your spirit simmers,
In the heat of your agony.
Not knowing when the burning will end,
We fuse new bonds with our shared suffering.

THE TUNNEL TRAVELERS
Ray Gehani

We are just traveling through,
The tunnel of our flesh and bones.
Like cars rushing through Holland Tunnel,
Going from Manhattan homes to Jersey shores.

We are just traveling through,
This toll tunnel of flesh and bones is not ours to keep.
We enter, we pay our toll, and we get out,
Our spirit lives and moves from this side to the other.

We are just traveling through,
With father, mother, son, daughter, and friend.
Traveling and talking with us for the journey
But our spirit will fly free and move on.

We are just traveling through,
Some cars are beside ours.
Others slightly ahead, or slightly behind.
We share the tunnel, but must leave it behind for more.

We are just traveling through,
Each mile differs; our road, traffic, and weather change.
We must live and stay engaged to the moment,
Not just where we have been, or where we are heading"home.

AUTUMN ANNOUNCES WINTER
Ray Gehani

My trees are decked in autumn lingerie
My paths are padded with fallen leaves
The autumn moon twinkles in the sky
To sneak a peek at the undressing tress.

Past spring was full of excitement
My summer sizzled with passion
It is time for autumn to ring time to retire
To get ready for much needed winter's sleep.

The winter birds are preparing
To take their long journey to warmer lands
They own nothing, they possess no homes
Feel abundance, make everywhere a home.

Punderson lake still rolls gently
Waves dance to Mother Nature's tunes
Soon winter will pull a white sheet over
To quiet down and contemplate within.

I come to lie in the lap of my loving lake
She puts me to sleep with her lullabies.
Calms down my storming frothy mind
Rejuvenates and vitalizes my tired soul.

MY LIFESPAN WITH PUNDERSON LAKE
Ray Gehani

In Summer Holidays
When Schools closed
As a Young Mother I brought my kids
To camp near your Lakeshore.

As my daughter and son grew older
They chased other boys and girls
They forgot about lakeshore
In search of distant pastures.

To share my solitude in middle age
I came back to sit at your side
I told you my complicated stories
Your waves patiently untangled my songs.

As I am getting old and frail
I still find in you a Best Friend
Your waves energize my ailing body
Your patient arms soar my soul.

HOLD ON
Ray Gehani

Hold on to our joy,
Even if it is just a faint after-taste.

Hold on to our dream,
Even if it seems too high to reach.

Hold on to our light,
Even if it is flickering in stormy winds.

Hold on to our promise,
Even if it is easier to let it break.

Hold on to our compassion,
Even if we seem alone in our premonition.

Hold on to our passion,
Even if we are consumed by our heightened flame.

Hold on to our love,
Even if it hurts to live in love.

Hold on to our memories,
Even when one person goes, our love endures.

OUR TOGETHERNESS
Ray Gehani

We pass our pain to and fro,
Through wireless waves across a big land.

We share, and split our pain to heal our wounds,
With tears falling like rain.

We taste together our bitterness,
And the emptiness of our gaping holes.

We fear our joy will come to a stop,
And we will miss being a full whole again.

We miss the time we lost,
When we could have made new memories.

We fear the time we would not have together,
When we could sing, dance, and drink.

But we are, we were, and we will always be a key part,
Of a universe that is, that was, and that will always be here.

LIFE GOES ON
Ray Gehani

I sat quietly
Did nothing
Spring came gently
And, the grass around me
Grew by itself.

Only the Tao
Or life Creating Spirit
Or that which is
Beyond Human Expression
Knows.

-Inspired By Basho

AT THE STREETSBORO LIGHT
Barbara M. Harkness

    MONDAY
Winter.
Waiting.
Cars ground in grime
Tires graveled with grit
Lanes walled by slush-slime-snow
      at corners and roadsides.
Waiting
for greenlight deliverance.

Meshed in a cloud of the bleak and barren
Segmented in the drone of everyday
    A dog,
    lies dead,
    astride the far lane.

The green blinks
Bliss!

Cars angrily swerve around the dog...
A stiffly dead dog
A heap on the asphalt of the dreary dull.

Lanes move in spurts and stretches
    Screeching, then forgetting
    The dog in soot and swill...
Nudging acceleration
To get to their
Wherevers

TUESDAY

Snow is black
Slush is saltier
Grey is greyer
Black is grey.
        The dog,
still dead
        Now tossed on the sooty snow
        along the side of the road
                out of the way
                        beneath the "no turn on red" sign.

Again
Delivered by greenlight
Cars zoom on to
The wherevers they're going.

WEDNESDAY

Rain
over grit and grime and gunk,
rain
that does not clean, nor clear, nor care.
Slush, slime, and salt oozes in the spaces
snow has smeared.
        The dog
still at the side of the road
        in the wet and the muck

                lies gently swaddled
                        in a faded drenched chenille bedspread,
                        cushioned on the flung crags of traffic
                        sleeping as the rain pours.

The greenlight startles

Cars move on

   Slowly

To the wherevers they're going.

                  THURSDAY
Hoping for a red light,
      Looking for the dog.

      Gone.

    The sun brightens the grime
    And halos the churned emptiness.

Cars move on.
Grinding the grit
To the wherevers they're going.

LYUBA
Barbara M. Harkness

Muck flowed into the trachea, filled the mouth, clogged the nostrils,
closed the cochlea,
Blinding the eyes
and stopping the lungs.
Groundless legs sank deeper
able only to churn.

She heard the fear-soaked bleating,
the choking fear, the suffocation.

Thrashing blades of sky-scraping grasses
snapping trees, crushing marshes
she trumpted her agony with trunk and feet.

She could go no further
on the viscous earth.
Frantically churning sedges and shrubs
into a muddy tangled desolation,
she shrieked at the sun and its impotence.
as the baby, with plaintive muffled weeping,
slipped into the abyss.

It disappeared in the ooze,
its trunk slowly yielding to swamp.

Others nuzzled her leathery sides
as the mother watched at what she had just given suck
vanish.

The others walked about and around
sometimes touching her gently
calling to her
in guttural grunts
that sang with their feet
as they moved in tandem.

They signaled to her as they moved on.
One or two looked back.

She stayed.

She vigiled her loss
as her cries became weak
and weakly become groans
and groans became whimpers.
She felt the skies darken,
Cooling the heat of her heaving.
The moon offered its benediction.
Still she stayed.
Shivers of whimpers rippled her hide
Until the first birds of morning
Announced 'light is coming'.
As it must.

Then she turned
to trail the herd that had slowly advanced.
No more crying
No more moaning.
She walked into the new day
and did not look back.

Without parameters of time or place
The super-collider of loss
drowns shrieks and screams of pain,
in the eternity of nanosphere.

Still the elephant bleats its loss.
The doe stands erect at the side of her dead fawn defying traffic
The gorilla carries the dead newborn until it stinks
Hopewell strews color over the child's cremation
Mary sobs at the base of the cross
The Incan mother swallows forbidden tears
Heaving over the pavement-flung pieces of her toddler
Mukama will not leave.

In the whirlwind of Hadron where there is no pain
Or loss
Or joy
Or delight
Collison collides
And collides.

Lyuba is a perfectly preserved baby mammoth carcass found by
reindeer hunters in Salekhard, Siberia in May, 2007. Probable age at
the time of death is one month. Although there is still some debate
as to whether she died in water or mud, apparently scientists do
agree that she died quickly and in her death she was submerged
in clay and silt. This sealed out oxygen and thwarted aerobic
microbes, both of which would otherwise have broken down soft
tissue. Other microbes containing lactic acid did invade her tissue,
"pickling" her carcass. Her age has been established at 40,000
years ago by Carbon-14 dating.

As the ground turned to permafrost, her body dehydrated and
she shrank to half her weight. In 2006 a river undercut the block
of permafrost containing Lyuba. The block melted, exposing her
body. Floodwaters washed it downstream to a sandbar. The
smell of lactic acid warded off scavengers. The Field Museum in
Chicago is planning an exhibit in 2010. Her name is that of Yuri
Khudi's wife. He and his sons were her discoverers. The May 2009
issue of <u>National Geographic</u> carries one of the many accounts of
her story.

FORGIVENESS
Cindy Hollis

I know, I no longer have to be perfect...
    To know His loving grace,
    To feel the warm embrace
  I had been missing all this time.

Although I feel that I will
    Stumble and fall...
    I will strive to do better
  While He patiently waits.

DEAR LORD,
Cindy Hollis

While bowing my head and asking for grace

Let me be responsive to:

      Recognizing without resignation
      Gratitude without attitude
      Rediscovering recovery
      Respect with dignity
      And finding gratitude with humility.

                Amen.

NEW DESTINATIONS
Cindy Hollis

Connecting one
Connecting two
impossibilities
and down the road
I go.

Envisioning one
Envisioning two
new possibilities
and down the road
I go.

CHANGE
Cindy Hollis

What you can't teach
You mustn't preach
But start within.
It's hard to reach.

It's spinning down
It's spinning around
It's looking up and
Starting anew.

It's working overtime
Down on my knees.
It's reaching
Teaching, preaching.

KATHLEEN

Bill Howland

I

I said to her, "In the past I frequently
became impatient with you.
Since we found out you have cancer
I never feel like that."

She said, "I have noticed.
This past year has been the
happiest year of my life."

I am very sorry that I did not
find her completely satisfactory.

And that she had to wait until
the last year of her life to
feel unqualified acceptance.

That was my loss.

II

She knew she was dying
And that death was near.
I knew dehydration was painful,
And that if she ate she would drink.

"Now, Kathleen, you have to eat something."
Her look was inscrutable.
Angry, but not really.
More like pretending to be angry
"Say, how would you like to live alone?
All by yourself?"

Why did she say that?
Was it because she was unhappy,
And wanted me to be unhappy?
Or was it a familiar pattern,
That somehow it was all my fault,

And that I should make everything right?
Although the words were hurtful
I treasure that memory.
I think she was so sure of my love
That she could say anything to me.

A few days later, the same entreaty
"Now, Kathleen, you have to eat."
"You're an asshole.
And don't you forget it."

Now I understand.
She was saying goodbye,
And making it easier
For me to say goodbye.

III

Although she died four months ago
I awaken each morning certain that she is by my side.
I reach out to pat her shoulder, her side, her bottom.
Then I am awake, with a terrible sense of loss.

I remember my recurring dream of being a small boy
Who has lost his precious beautiful marble.
And the horrible certainty that I will never again
Fall asleep with her head on my shoulder.

IV

I keep thinking that there is something
I have forgotten to do.
Oh yes. I was supposed to meet Kathleen.
But I can't. Kathleen is dead.
She has been dead these last two years.
Does this recurring feeling mean
That now I am forgetting Kathleen?

Or does it mean that I will soon be meeting her again?

39

THE WIND AND THE RIVER

Bill Howland

The river flows from the past
Through the present
On its way to the future.
The river and the wind run together,
But the wind may exist only for the moment.

The river talks to the wind
And the wind answers her.
They talk about
Where they've been
And where they're going.

They talk about the
Good things they've seen
And forsake the tragic
And the evil.

Sometimes the wind
Makes the river angry, and
They shout at each other.

But when the river is calm
She trembles,
As the wind touches her.

40

MY NAME WAS JOY

Bill Howland

My mother called me, "Billy Joy."
"You are my pride and joy."
But my friends laughed at my name.

My father was dying.
"Billy, there is something I must tell you.
Your middle name is not 'Joy.'
Joy was the name of my girlfriend
For many years before I met your mother.
We promised that we would
Name our first child after each other.

But I couldn't betray your mother
By giving her what she wanted.
I spared her the hurt of truth.

Your middle name is 'J.'
Promise you won't ever tell your mother."
For all of her life,
My mother called me, "Billy Joy."

THE WHY OF DO

Bill Howland

A shadowy room exists in my brain,
I can only occasionally enter,
When falling asleep or on first awakening.
Over the entrance is written in ancient script:
THE WHY OF DO.

Once inside I can climb
In the huge pile of charred lumber.
I can see the pictures and read the writings
That are engraved in the wood.

Sometimes it is clear, but usually not.
The fire has burned away important things.
They may make me happy, but more often sad.
I can carry only small pieces outside.

On a recent evening
I found a piece that I could carry out,
Why I became a doctor.

When I was a small child I brought
A little chick back to life
By gently pushing on its chest.

A few minutes later the chick died
And would not come back to life.
If only I knew more.

The pictures showed me that
The chick was buried
With its beak out of the ground,
In case it came back to life.
That was the Why of Do.

ANDREW JAMES, A.J.
Nathalie Ketterer

All day I had been
a crystal bell ringing: he's coming
he's coming…he's coming.
He's here!

His baby blue blanket
Is cowled over his head
against the ardent sun.
Then wispy light hair appears
and a dear pink face
with chubby cheeks.
Eyes shut with itty-bitty lashes
open their blue.
He makes a newborn's mystic,
cute face, my grandson,
and I lift him into my life.

MY CAROUSEL
Nathalie Ketterer

Off you would go in the mist of day,
Never, never to know
How I loved you...
            from *Carousel* by Rodgers & Hammerstein

We cross the field of pain together,
I with my fibrillating heart,
you with your lupus.
It is the violet hour, and the evening
star appears, punctual over pines.
A small stream whispers,
and from the rumpled weeds
there is a thin, persistent music
of grasshoppers and crickets.

Defying the dark grave, we hold
each other, mother and daughter,
as knowingly as roses and grapevines,
climbing the same sun-hot trellis.
Smiles dissolving,
at the bottom of the dream
we cry for where we had
never voyaged before.

A REMOTE COUNTRY
Nathalie Ketterer

Sitting on the porch, in the pall
of the yellow light bulb,
we tore open our secrets,
which boys we liked,
how we could get them
to notice us,
what we would do with them
when we grew up.

Populating my universe
was Joe,
a lofty eighth grader.
Betty had Steve of the
incessant smile.

From the movies
we learned about love,
a remote country
like China or Connecticut.
We entreated the moon.
But the cool night only flew
against the windows
in moths and crickets.

Relapsing into silence,
staring at the stars
through broken light and shadow
we could only yearn
toward the proscenium
that framed the luminous world
beyond the porch.

HOLOCAUST MUSEUM
Nathalie Ketterer

Washington, D.C.

I was broken into pieces
  as I came out of that place.
    Everywhere there had been
      stick figures

like the first scrawling of children.
  Only these were real people once,
    ripped from a green summer,
      shoved into viscous dark,

and shipped to landlords
  of a unique killing field.
    Death came into my quiet.
      I will always see the shoes

all sizes, broken, moldy
  the eye glasses, knives, forks
    and at the end...
      the hair, the hair!

INTIMATION OF WINTER
Nathalie Ketterer

Sometimes she unzips
her briefcase and finds
blood at the bottom.
Each morning she is
nailed into place and
wonders what
she is doing here
in a room with no door.
Spring shuts
behind her back.

Today she made up
carefully with Clinique,
the woman who
had once been young and
said to have genius.
On her desk the flowers,
as well, wait in the vase,
their fugitive colors dying.

She can raise questions
that are close
to the bone.

AT THE HIGH SCHOOL
Nathalie Ketterer

There's a flurry of leaves against my window;
autumn, a bright new semester has begun.
Only, in Mentor, at the high school, the scene
was set for Greek tragedy. He took a gun
in his hand and fired an exit for himself.
To the desolations of a wailing rock star on
the DVD, another swallowed all of his mother's
pills. A third, when she looked in the mirror
and saw the clothes she hated, along with
her snarled Ophelia hair, hung herself.

They were too skinny, too fat, too weird,
too silent, always too something.
Certain other students just threw them away.
All three were bullied at school and on line, discussed,
and laughed at in contemptuous whispers.

My granddaughter, who went to school in
Mentor, confirmed there were the haves
and the have-nots. The have-nots, who were bullied,
dwelled in bleak rooms webbed in shadow, and
the night finally closed down on them.
Their headlines clot in my blood.

Prodigal Son
(a father's view)
Phyllis Lee

Prodigal sons
are supposed to come to their senses
before returning home.
You arrive senseless, after seven years,
with half-mast eyes and two bags
of ripe laundry.

We watch you go to the kitchen.
(You must have practiced walking straight
for occasions such as these.)
It is the air around you that staggers—
weaves its way to our nostrils.

Your mother asks if you want hot bread
and noodles. All you want is the crooked couch
in the crooked basement
until the crooked divorce is final.

For weeks now, I have watched your mother's heart
open and close, like the mouth of a fish
before dying. She croons to you from the upright—
Jesus loves me, this I know;
shows you photographs from your good-boy days.
You in your fire truck (real steel), smiling
big enough to make your eyes close.

Some days, she gets tough—gives ultimatums.
Clean your own ashtrays. Read the books from AA
in three days, or else!
Last night I heard her pray God's spirit into
your last bottle of Stroh's. After your shower,

you went for it, passed it from hand to hand,
then put it back for being too warm.

We fight over who's to blame.
She says I was too hard on you—should have
quit my cursing and repented years ago.
I say she should have let me brain you
in the beginning, like when you shot out
the basement window with your BB gun.

She doesn't know half the uptown stories
I have kept from her in my secret keg, fermenting.
She said she would leave me if I put you out.
I must take that chance.
If you need her, she won't be hard to find.
Look for a woman in some small yard.
She will be the one hoeing stones for bread,
humming hymns,
tending the fatted calf.

IN WRITING I HAVE COME

Joseph McLaughlin

in writing i have come
to meet the self
wrapped like a mummy
in colorful rags
i thought to make
a piece of literature
but was not ready
to make one brick
for the cathedral
all that i have done
amounts to a single grain
of sand
ungathered
on a vast, windswept
beach
where the self
wanders by, brown feet
splashed by the moving
edge of tide,
leaving a trail of marks
two feet, one stick
for it is a long
eternal walk
and the gulls cry out
in heart language
to be, to be

PHILOSOPHICAL QUESTIONS AND ANSWERS
Joseph McLaughlin

"There is only one law— the law of cause and effect."
—Swami Sivananda

I
what if we stopped
imposing our wills
on one another?

this gray, winter day
would burst into sunshine

II
what if we stopped hating our neighbors,
poisoning wells,
stealing firewood?

the crows on the roof
would fly off in protest

III
what if this ego
were no longer an ego,
but the scent of a rose?

eternal spring
would rise up
like a green giant

IV
what if we stepped back
from the end of the world?

then god would awaken
smile big, show
his golden tooth

MEMO TO DESIRE

Joseph McLaughlin

I

soft sigh of desire
you ask so much
in a whisper
to breathe
the rose perfume
without the pain of thorn
to see the crescent moon
fall from the sky
and break at your feet
it is the pang of loss
you cherish, the melancholy
pool of silence it brings
so you begin with the ads
in the morning papers,
mail stuffed with possibilities
from these you make
long lists which can never
be fulfilled

II

you wear the ever-changing
mask of desire
which lives in you like a second soul
desire illuminates your dark eyes,
quickens your pace, your speech
even as it intoxicates
it is desire which reaches out
to touch the silver cloth
spread before you

paints your face
in tribal colors
and patterns
leads you to enter
the mating dance around
the great midnight fire
O warble to us now, dressed
in green bird feathers,
tell us what you see

THE DANGERS OF PROPHECY
Joe McLaughlin

Sitting at a cafe inside the city wall,
I wrote down ten fragments
carelessly selected from my journal.
Those around me thought it was scripture.
A crowd gathered–veiled women,
men flapping dusty robes, naked children.
"Who are you?" demanded an old graybeard.
Wary and amazed, my smile froze on my face.
"Give him a white robe," someone shouted,
"so we can honor him!" "And thorns," cried another.
Like Roberto Benigni accepting with a joke
his second Oscar for *Life is Beautiful,*
I tried to explain: "There's been a terrible mistake..."
The crowd swirled and parted.
An archer stepped into the void,
bow drawn, arrow aimed at my heart.
My friends tackled me just as its song
whistled over my head, hurried me away
toward a donkey. "No, you don't," I yelled.
"I'll take my chances with the jackals outside!"

54

UNTITLED 1
Kevin O'Brien

Would that the selling of hugs
Be as lucrative
As the selling of arms.

Would we still be the richest country?

Christian values aside
We'd rather shake on a deal
Than shake on a friendship.

There is security in strength
Christian values aside.

UNTITLED 2
Kevin O'Brien

The existential dilemma is:
How do I enter
And enjoy the present moment
When,
At the same time,
My sisters and brothers
Are in such pain?

Being both solitary
And one with all
The question is not
Who am I;
It is,
How am I?

MAHATMA
Kevin O'Brien

With each peaceful step
This man of no consequence
Became The Great One.

UNTITLED 3
Kevin O'Brien

They jump on treadmills
And Stairmasters
In their vain attempt to get in shape –
Trying to get ahead or climb
Their way up ultimately to nowhere.

Blessed is the gardener
Who steps, bends and lifts
Thinking not of themselves
But the wonder of nature
And, in the process,
Feeds their souls
While loosing some weight.

UNTITLED 4
Kevin O'Brien

Who will sit with me and speak of things of soul?
To question my thoughts of truth and rightness?
Who will encourage me to think deeper
And so transform my life into something not mediocre?

Who has time to sit idly by and listen
Who still wonders and wanders looking for something
Or someone who will elicit his own answers?

Who has an empty agenda and patiently listens to mine?
Who has a body still able to move
And react with a cougar's swiftness?
Where are the sages of the past –
The kind I read now on modern art?
Who has the imagination to create a concrete dream
In a world that rewards practicality?
Who will inspire our better angels
And thus transform the world?

UNTITLED HAIKU
Valentina Ranaldi-Adams

two vivid birds perch
in a small tree now laid bare
by winter's approach

        electric lines snap
        bushes bend and trees uproot
        storm of heavy ice

envelope with your
Valentine card I leave on
mausoleum floor

        loud explosive sound
        lightning strikes two tall poplars
        a squirrel lies dead

UNTITLED HAIKU
Valentina Ranaldi-Adams

on top of white snow
colorful Easter eggs lie
for children to find

> gold leaves on tree are
> identical to brown ones
> lying on the ground

police sirens howl
as neighborhood church bells ring
to mark the half-hour

ABSTRACT ART
Sam Rettman

Strange, whenever
I look
at a woman now,

I see her
as she is.
But as suddenly

as wind shifts
on late
fall afternoons,

the image
is transformed.

You have invaded
my viewing
of the picture, and

although it warms me
to see you
alive again,

my moment
in the gallery
has been ruined.

BEFORE DAWN
Sam Rettman

Suddenly,
in the leaden western sky
the moon drops from behind a curtain of low clouds
and floats toward the horizon.
Despite a yellowed document asleep in the bedroom desk
that suggests I'm an educated man,
I simply can not comprehend how this pale egg,
perched on the crest of a road my car is climbing,
reflects light from a sun not yet announced in the east.

Suddenly.
it seems to breath with an energy entirely its own.
Suddenly,
it is not the cold, barren ball
whose recognition has depended since creation,
as I have been led to believe,
on the warring flames of a distant star.
A surge of acceleration buoys me,
as though the car has lifted off and is streaking upward,
unsaddled from the road,
from suggestion,
from comprehension,
from belief,
racing to crash the radiant pearl
before the sky is empty again.

61

DUMB BIRDS

Sam Rettman

When I slid my arm
around the silky band
of your pink prom dress,
our hips locked
like a zipper.
We strolled
through the dim corridor
(scarred gray lockers lined its walls)
into the Big Dipper night.
I breathed
the soft tension of you;
you breathed mine.
Innocent and alone
as two doves
riding an oak branch.

GAP-TOOTHED TRANSFORMATION

Sam Rettman
I don't climb the stairs
two at a time anymore.

Well, at least if I start to,
I catch myself.

As though my teeth have shrunk,
I no longer devour the apple.

Now I bite off less than I can chew,
only nibbles, like a narcotized rabbit.

Lately I've noticed even the spaces
between my words have widened.

The kitten in me has renounced its friskiness.
My litter-flinging days are over.

62

THE WALNUT TREE

Sam Rettman

Across the road he stands,
tall and straight,
his bare limbs
silhouette a frosted sky.
Retreating from the cold sun,
his lifeblood creeps
like a shadow,
down through the rings
that celebrate his existence,
back to his roots.
Imperturbable,
he braces for the onslaught.
Seasons of experience
have taught him he can survive.
A magnificent spirit
will likely liberate
his verdant energy again.
But now, as I press my brow
against the fogged glass,
I see only naked branches.
They are a tangle of dark bones.

A TAO GHAZAL

Inder Shah

Translated from the Gujarati by the author

Effortlessly like a fish I swim naturally;
Naturally live I and die I naturally.

Wherever the wind takes it the leaf floats on thither;
I will go wherever you take me and move about naturally.

Thoughts take me to the past and to the future;
Standing still in the "here and now," I stay naturally.

What is expressed in words is never ever the truth;
In the bottomless depth of silence I descend naturally.

What is unbending will surely break, but I shall bow down;
Let the whole world win, I accept defeat naturally.

NEW ADAM

Inder Shah

Translated from the Gujarati by the author

From the womb of the Earth,
The New Adam of the twenty-first century
Has been born.

These Tsunami earthquakes,
Tornadoes, cyclones, storms are
But the wails of giving birth.

The seething lava of anger
In his heart
Has cooled down.
He will now not need
To fight wars
For catharsis.
Terrorism will now come to an end.
A new day will break.
Everywhere will spread
The light of awareness.
He will obey only one command –
That of his own conscience.
His ethics will be personal,
Not social.
He will not be a Hindu, Muslim, Jewish
Or the follower of Christ.

THE PROPHET

Joe Torma

They stopped and stared as he passed by
          with purpose quite apart
And they tried to scratch the finish
          from his memory and his heart
But he'd a suit of nonchalance
          bedecked with peaceful pose
And carried news of ugliness
          as if it were a rose.
"What odd manner, what strange style"
          were comments that he heard
As he stretched a groping hand
          and stuttered stilted words.
Men like him have passed their way
          and played their foolish games
While all the while remembering
          the reason why they came.
He'd scream with agony at times
          with terror-twisted mind
At seeing all the broken brains
          and all the eyes gone blind.
He gasped when clearness washed away
          the illusion of import
And then he grasped the message
          that had swallowed up his word—
"The world to which you're burden
          must shake you from its back."
And all too soon he too was pressed
          to waver and give slack;
But stoned by silent missiles
          and drained by empty smiles
He played their game while teaching his
          and crawling lonely miles.

ANTIQUE DESK
Caroline Totten

In the evening light,
it is like a memory
filled with empty pigeon holes;
it promises nothing,
it is a home that waits
for the daily mail.
The voices returning.

It notices
the sharp opener is lost
the countless pens dried to invisible,
the sudden gripping of hands on the edge–
it hears the words,

scratching
at the dark mahogany
in which wood knots blossom
into spirals of hollyhocks
for those who wait and age,
like wood, patient with change,
shaped and polished by death.

MEANDER
Carolyn A. Weldon

Towpath Trail/Cuyahoga Valley

I pause to catch my breath
on the footbridge spanning the Cuyahoga
between the gray, shale cliff
and the venerable sycamores on the opposite bank.
Where the sun sounds the depths, the river
is as clear as green tea;
the shade obscures all colors but its own.

Upstream, the water sweeps around a bend.
Swimming with the flow,
a long, slow, curve of snake
consumes the current
at a cool, reptilian rate.
Even if I wanted to, I couldn't look away.
I cross to the other rail to watch it
make its way downstream.
Two wanderers, we share the same disdain
for the straight line. The water snake
rests its length of spring-loaded muscle
on a shelf of submerged shale – its body
mottled with colors riverine,
its narrow head above the waterline.
After a moment, the snake slides downstream.
and is lost to me in the cliff's deep shadow.

I can't help thinking ahead
to a time when the snake will be
tangled on a snag in the river,
a rag of skin – scaled and abraded –
a spine uncoiled, ribs sprung, bleached bone
leaching into the current.

No need to follow this line of thought
all the way to the inevitable, Better to imagine
the river taking all the time it needs
to carve its name into the land.
The serpentine existence
of snake and woman amounts to nothing more
than ripples on the surface of
the Crooked River.

THE BIG BOYS

Carolyn A. Weldon

I-40/ Oklahoma

Hearts of diesel,
clatter and snarl
of engines restless for
the Interstate.
Every color on the wheel,
milling the parking lot.
Earth–shakers, fire-breathers,
their breath corrodes the sun.
Turbo-whine rises out of
their gravity.
All chrome and *cojones,*
they bellow their own mythology
at us mortals down here
hugging the blacktop.
No wonder they act like
they own the road.

Thunderheads blacken
Tornado Alley.
Tracer lightning,
strafe of hail.
The Big Boys
strap on their running lights,
and storm the storm:
thunder for thunder,
backhanding rain,
parting the waters,
and their eyes
are on fire.

HINDSIGHT
Carolyn A. Weldon

A Tale of Two Sisters

Every time I saw you two together
your sister was backed into a corner.
A woman who wears her heart on her sleeve
is as easy to play
as third-desk triangle
in a first-grade rhythm band.
And play her you did –
against the neighbors, her husband,
her children.
You fed her rumor and suggestion:
the misinformation she Needed To Know.
All those years you lavished loving
control
on Little Sister,

until the night

God said,
"ENOUGH ALREADY!"

or

two lilies and a headstone
came up on the Big Slot Machine,

or

Sister's heart decided to go
"Bang!"

And she left you

twisting
your hanky
at the funeral.

TRINITY

Carolyn A. Weldon

When the first atomic bomb was detonated at
Trinity Site, in New Mexico, the intense heat
melted the desert sand, creating a new element:
the radioactive glass, Trinitite.

You pick tiny wildflowers
near the site of Trinity,
where "death, the destroyer
of worlds" escaped its creators
to rampage in the desert–never
looking back on its cloven hoofprints
fused in glass.

You hold the flowers
gently in your weathered hands,
offering me these microcosms
of petal and leaf
as proof that there is no such thing
as death.

"Or, we can fight
fire with fire," I say.
I begin to stroke
you, stoke you
up; and we raise
a minor rampage
of our own.

When the rains come,
wildflowers will
carouse
in our footprints.

TIME CHANGE
Carolyn A. Weldon

It's the last evening the sun's allowed
to stay up late. Tonight's the night
they kick the daylights
out of Daylight Savings Time,
they presume to tinker
with the speed of light,
pushing whole populations
into the past.

The owl lives in *real* time—
no yesterdays, and no tomorrows;
the raptor knows darkness
falls when it falls.
Twin talons of light, his eyes
reflect the crescent moon.
Instinct screams at the mouse,
foraging for beechnuts on the forest floor,
in time to flee descending wings.
While human time moves"click
by digital click"toward 6:00 a.m. alarm,
the garrulous sparrows
pick up their bickering
exactly where they dropped it
at sunset.

BELLS
Theresa Woods

Ring a bell?
Carillon or belfry
iron strong like liberty bells.
War bells
Latin bellum
peace bells ring too seldom.
Glass bells
ceramic bells
metal bells.
High pitch, low pitch
Reminds me of
Hand bells.
Love to play them.
Silver bells
city bells
sleigh ride bells
reindeer bells
Cat bells shaped like
Jingle bells
Run mouse run
Hear those church bells.
Wedding bells
Golden anniversary bells
Wonder why no funeral bells
Slow and steady low tones
For whom the bell tolls bells
Now bellowing homeward
how now brown cow
country cow bells
sturdy like Buddha bells
calling now, now, now.
Clock bells
Flower bells
gracing meadows
Lilly of the Valley brushing hems of
Bell-bottom jeans strolling through
summertime bluebells

while the bellbird calls
as delicate as the belle of the ball
coos at the bell hop.
Who dreams of putting her in a bell jar
To keep forever?
Ship bells
Bell man echos bell bouy warning
through rain drenched boulevard
hungry for hot bell peppers.
Dinner bells
Door bells
Timer bells
and that dreaded alarm clock bell
enough to make one bellicose
Unless one wants to shop for souvenir bells.
Crocheted bells,
embroidered bells,
camel bells
as the desert swells
precious few bells in the Bible
robe of the ephod
holy garment
alternating bell of pure gold and pomegranate.
Zechariah
Inscribed on the bells of the horses: "Holy to the Lord"
Clay bells
Wooden bells
Pewter bells
Bicycle bells
Counter top bells that don't look like bells.
tap the top, here comes help, hip hop.
You rang?

SEPTEMBER SHOE TIME
Theresa Woods

It's time for the flip flops to rest.
One atop the other,
flipped heel to toe,
flopped on top a shoe box,
gathering dust,
remembering soft soil they pathed through gardens
and gritty gravel walks down the driveway
and back again bearing the added weight of packages.

Then down steep basement steps where
heavy boots await winter snow drifts.
Side by side, heel to heel, toe to toe, ready.
As if they could hear the autumn rain whispering
"Passing through, just passing through."

Whose shoes? My shoes? Choose shoes.
A pair for this dress. A pair for those slacks.
One pair for these old work clothes.
A pair for walking and one for weeding
and loafers just because I liked them
when I saw them on sale last spring.

October will be here tomorrow; shuffling in
like old tan corduroy slippers,
crinkling like dry leaves, and soft as, well,
soft as autumn rain.

Creative Non-Fiction

LIFE LESSONS FROM A DOLL NAMED EDITH
Deanna R. Adams

I'm waiting in the long line at the bookstore so I could surprise my 11-year-old with a coveted copy of the latest Harry Potter book. I hate standing in line. I always think of other things I could be doing. But this time I don't mind. It's for a worthwhile cause. This simple act of standing in line to purchase a book is part of my legacy to my daughter. More than any other material possession I may leave her, I hope it is the books she'll treasure most. The books that, as an adult, will take her back to the times her mother read to her, or what is now more the case, the times spent reading in solitude in her bedroom, or on the couch with a blanket on a rainy day.

I'm standing in line because I want to pass down to my children my inherent love of books and the magic they produce. Magic that far exceeds even a spark of Harry Potter's wand. It is indeed magic when you can open a book and find yourself suddenly transported to fascinating places. It's magical to become friends with intriguing characters, who become a part of our lives. My generation grew up reading about some unforgettable protagonists who we readily identified with. The boys imagined being Huckleberry Finn, Superman, or the Hardy Boys. Girls fantasized about being Anne of Green Gables, Nancy Drew, or one of the Little Women (for me, a writer in the making, was always Jo).

Those characters ultimately provided lasting memories we now share with those who have taken that same journey. Before I had even met Jo, however, there was Edith. I was seven when I received *The Lonely Doll Learns a Lesson*, by Dare Wright. I know this because the inscription inside: "Merry Christmas, Dee Dee, 1961." I may have abandoned that nickname long ago, but Edith has had a lasting impact.

For some reason the gift giver didn't sign her name (it's definitely a woman's handwriting) so I'm not sure who gave me that wonderful book those many years ago. I wish I did. Forty years later, I'd love to tell her how her gift enriched my childhood, and now, that of my children. And how, amazingly, it's one of the few books of mine that survived all the various residences and changes that make up one's journey into adulthood. Until I had children, the book remained packed away in a box that moved from apartment to apartment, house to house, for decades. Although I rarely gave

Edith much thought then, I knew, like a treasured childhood friend, I'd never abandon her. But of course, as I grew, I went on to other literary works. I fell in love with other authors, I admired other characters. But wherever I went in life, Dare Wright's Edith was there, waiting patiently for me to rediscover her.

My children were two and five when I realized it was time to reacquaint myself with my first literary friend. I sat my little ones down for story time, and went to find her, anxiously sifting through the archives of my youth. Sure enough, the book, a bit tattered but intact, was there, tucked away at the bottom of a pile of my favorite childhood things. Goose bumps bubbled up as I pulled out the oversized book, recalling the joy of reading it as a young girl. Dare Wright was the first author who gave me a real love for the written word and showed me the creative ways in which it can be used. A professional photographer, Wright used black-and-white photographs as illustrations, showing a pretty doll, stuffed bears, and a live kitten to depict her characters of Edith, Big Bear, Little Bear and the pet that threatened Edith and Little Bear's friendship. As a result, all characters seemed as if they could walk right out of the pages.

The story was meaningful, yet light, unlike those Grimm's fairy tales (how appropriate the name . . .) I was so used to. In her brilliant photographs, the innovative author placed the characters in various positions and scenes that created the accurate response or emotions of the tale. It was different from any other book I'd ever read–before or since.

As I sat on that couch, a child on each side, and read this book to my little girls, I was carried–magically–back in time. Back to a time when everything seemed simpler. Black and white. Like the 12-inch television in my childhood home. Back when life's lessons seemed easier to learn. Lessons like, if you don't have anything nice to say, don't say anything at all. Or don't forget to say thank you. Or never tell a lie.

The moral of Wright's story was that, although Edith got a new playmate, a cute cuddly little kitten, she shouldn't abandon or ignore her old faithful friend, Little Bear.

"When you were lonely, Edith, who was your first friend?" asked Big Bear.

"Little Bear," admitted Edith.

"A new friend is a fine thing but that's no reason to neglect an old friend."

That one conversation between Edith and Big Bear emphasized our human need for companionship and compassion, and underlined the true meaning of friendship. It also served as a reminder that being considerate of others benefits us as well. That the more friends we make in our lives, the better. A valuable lesson for adults as well as children.

Not long after I stood in that line to purchase the latest installment of J. K. Rowling's tome, I read that Dare Wright had died. I was surprised by my sadness. I didn't know her, never knew what became of her after she completed "The Lonely Doll" series. Yet I felt a personal loss. The loss of a true childhood companion. With news of this author's death, I mourned her because she was one of the least connections to the girl I once was. A personal loss indeed.

Yet I was also in for a surprise. As I read Dare Wright's obituary, I learned that she had grown up in my hometown of Cleveland. Her still-life photographs of Edith were of Wright's own doll that her mother had bought her at Halle's downtown department store. The same store I myself had visited often throughout my childhood. That huge and exciting store that was also the holiday home of Mr. Jingling, "the keeper of Santa's keys."

I also discovered that the other characters in her books, Big Bear and Little Bear, represented Wright's father and brother who remained in her native Ontario, after her parents divorced when she was five. Somehow, all this information emphasized the loss. Wright and I shared not only the vision of being a writer, but also hometown landmarks. Her childhood memories paralleled my own. I felt closer to this exceptional author. I suddenly longed to meet her. To stand in line to purchase her other books. To speak to her, as she has spoken to me through Edith. Now I would never have that chance. Had I known these personal details as a child, I would have treasured the book all the more.

Well, maybe not. After all, the story had already endeared itself to me from that Christmas day I received it. And I'm sure those goose bumps wouldn't have happened upon retrieving it from the box, had I not put the book out of sight–and out of mind. For in packing away this book I loved as a child, I was able to pack away those wonderful memories along with it. To save for a rainy day. To retrieve in a time when life was no longer black and white, no longer simple. And later, to read to my children and give them a part of my own childhood.

The day after hearing that sad news, I sat my kids down and read *The Lonely Doll* in Wright's honor. And suddenly it was 1961 and Edith was teaching me about considering other's feelings and how to be a good friend. But she was also teaching me how to be a good mother to my Little Women.

There's another lesson we learned that day, that books entertain us in many lasting ways. That our beloved childhood heroes, be it dolls or bears or wizards, and those who create them, have enduring worth that live on in the reader's heart.

We learned, too, that authors, through their prose, have much to teach us. About life. About friendship. About the magic of books.

I suspect Dare Wright knew that all along.

SISTER OF AN ONLY CHILD
Judi Christy

My sister is an only child. I am too. True, we have the same parents, the same maiden names, the same catechistical upbringing that serves guilt with its meat and potatoes. Yet, I always think of Joanna and me as being raised alone. She is my only sibling and 16 years my senior.

Joanna and I never had pillow fights or races to grab the phone. We didn't do each other's hair, wear each other's clothes or share each other's dreams. I didn't know her secret crushes, her favorite movie star, or the way she *really* felt about Mom and Dad. She didn't know that I thought she was pretty, wished I had her teeth instead of mine, or envied the way she could sing "People" and sound just like Barbara Streisand.

Joanna and I didn't exchange passwords or glances, homework assignments, or life lessons learned.

I was a kid. She was a woman.

The year I started first grade, Joanna got married. My mom said that Joanna fell in love with the boy next door. To me, Bill was just another adult.   He seemed okay, smiled when I baked him chocolate cake from my Easy Bake oven, and bought me Coke and popcorn when the three of us saw *The Sound of Music*.

In later years, when Joanna and her husband went to the cinema alone,   I would watch their daughter, feed her with a Mother Goose spoon and pretend that I was the lady of the house. I sometimes tried on Joanna's "teacher" clothes or her makeup, a dime store array of colors and smells not permitted for little girls who lived alone with Mom and Dad. *Did I really want to be like her?*

I didn't think so. Married. Babied. Bored. I was a teenager who knew everything about nothing and nothing about life.

My parents were older, more tired and more tolerant.   They left me alone while they golfed and socialized, bought me a car for my 16th birthday and told me to behave until they got home from work. In turn, I cleaned the toilets, learned how to make dinner and found that solitude was something I enjoyed. I wrote poetry and dreamt of marrying Joe Namath. I sang alto in our high school choir and rode my 10-speed bike to the pool every day in the summer.

Joanna swam there too. Confined to the baby pool, another child now in her belly, she waved to me at the deep end and bought me an ice cream sandwich at least once a week. Some of my new friends thought she was my mother. I don't remember if I told them she was not.

But, I do remember crying when she moved. Her husband's job went south, so Joanna became a rebel. At least to my parents. She had always done the right thing, at least until now, and they resented that she left. They didn't tell her though. But I knew. I got a new Camero the summer she drove away. I never had the chance to take her for a ride.

I was 18 and starting college; Joanna was 34 and starting over.

Months later, my grandmother died. And I was here to comfort my mother. I was here when she turned 60 and when my father decided that it was best if he retired. I was here to plan my parents' anniversaries at 40 years and 50, sit by their sides through surgeries and roll my eyes daily at their hard-of-hearing questions. I was here to fall in love, marry the boy my parents disliked and get a great job with a great company.

But, Joanna was here too. Sort of. At least through cards and telephone talk. Her words were liquid, easy to hear, easy to erase.

She had her own life. And, I had mine. A daughter. A wife. A fast-tracker. A mother?

I was 31. She was 47. For both of us, the results were in: Positive.

Our doctor's appointments were 750 miles apart. I had gained 50 pounds. Joanna had lost weight. My due date was in November, the big day for Joanna would come after Christmas.

I had a daughter who was healthy and new. Joanna's healthy son was now a new father.

At miles apart WalMarts, we both bought Pampers and playpens, car seats with safety latches and out-of-season outfits that we could save till next year. I quit my job and Joanna changed hers. We had new responsibilities; new babies to raise. New ground to cover.

We talked more frequently, discussed measles shots and diarrhea and what was up with Barney. We compared growth charts and teething tantrums, new fangled thermometers and bedtime routines that changed every night.

Joanna and I consoled each other through potty training. Patted our faraway backs at each new word spoken. Both of our babies were geniuses, super models, and best-in-show all around. Because mine was a girl and hers was a boy, they didn't compete. Only children, like these, could indeed have it all.

I certainly did. I never had to share my toys or my room. I made my own choices and mistakes. I had no one to blame but myself.

Today I am 43; Joanna is 59. When I look in the mirror, I see her. Laugh lines, deep set eyes, a thought that is far away. When Joanna talks on my machine, her voice is mine. Fast, no drawl, words that jam together before the cut-off beep.

How are things? Mom and Dad?

Hers or mine? I wonder.

Joanna and I have the same parents. We have the same maiden name. We have the same Catholic hang-ups, fear of our father's temper and secret desire to be thinner than our 80-year-old mother.

When I think of Joanna, I wonder if her life will be mine. Will my husband wander to other interests? Will my clothing catch-on to middle age? Will my perfect child have a perfect child? Will someone call me Grandma when I have yet to turn grey? Will my smile thin, then fade to frown?

Other sisters could ask for clues, for signs, for sibling-centered hope. But we cannot. We are not that type of kin. Joanna and I have never shared secrets, had pillow fights, or told each other how we *really* feel.

We are just two grown up women, living miles apart, years away. Sisters connected by a blood line that is so transparent, its knot can slip with one single pull.

HER EYES WERE BLUE
Bill Howland

My best friend Bobby was keeping me company while we bicycled on my paper route. After I threw the paper to a house on the edge of town he said, "Say, did you know that old Mrs. Wirth knew Jessie James?"

The next day I knocked on her door and said, "Mrs. Wirth, would you tell me about Jesse James?" She hesitated and looked at me for what seemed like a long time and then said, "Well Billy, I guess it has been long enough ago that I can tell you about him. You come back after you have finished your route. I baked some sugar cookies today and we'll sit down and have some cookies and milk."

I hurried through the rest of my route. Mrs. Wirth lived in an old farmhouse. It was typical of Kansas's farmhouses, being one and one-half stories with weather-beaten wood siding. There were a few acres of land with an old chicken house and a barn. I knew she kept chickens and one cow, which she milked twice a day, although she was in her eighties. The roofed front porch had two doors leading into the house. The one on the left opened to the front parlor and the one on the right to the large kitchen.

When I walked into the kitchen I was most impressed by a large, heavy oak table with three wooden chairs on each side and large armchairs at each end. I knew that her children had left home long ago and that she lived alone. When I looked at Mrs. Wirth she said, "This is the table where Jesse and his friends sat. I keep it like this because you never know who is going to drop in." There were cookies and milk on the table.

As I looked around I could see a large, wood burning cook stove and two massive oak cabinets. The floor was covered with linoleum, faded and cracked. At the sink was a hand pump.

Mrs. Wirth was rather plump. Her eyes were blue. They had not aged like the rest of her body but were bright and expressive, especially when she smiled. She was quick and efficient in her talk and manner. She was dressed in a white apron with red flowers and a checked red and blue dress. I recognized the material from feed sacks. At that time livestock feed came in cloth that could be used to sew clothes. My mother had made me a shirt out of the same checked cloth that I refused to wear.

"Yes, Jessie and his gang were frequently here. You see, my husband Carl was a cousin to Cole and Bob Younger. We had only been married a few weeks the first time they came. Carl had told me about them so it wasn't a big surprise, but I was kind of scared. I was only seventeen. I was blonde and I knew I was pretty. I had heard a lot of stories about the James-Younger gang. This was the summer of 1874. They had already robbed a lot of banks and trains and killed a lot of people."

I knew that this small Kansas town was close to the Missouri border and that after the Civil War there were lots of southern sympathizers in the area. Many felt that Jessie and his gang were just taking back from the northerners what they had taken away from the southerners.

Mrs. Wirth ate a cookie and continued.

I can remember that first visit like it was yesterday. Carl introduced each one of them to me, starting with Jesse, then Frank, Cole and Bob, and four others whose names I can't remember. It was early in the morning, still dark out. They had been riding all night and were dusty and dirty and smelled like horse sweat. They all wore dusters, which they carefully folded and stacked in a corner. They all wore guns, which they didn't take off, but they did stack their rifles in the same corner.

"I started making coffee and breakfast, using two of my biggest skillets to fry pork chops and eggs and putting a big batch of biscuits in the oven. Carl took two of the men out to help him do the morning chores. We had a big farm then. After Carl died I had to sell off most of the land. Jessie sat down in the chair you're sitting in, which was closest to the stove, and watched me work. When I occasionally glanced back I could see in his eyes that he wasn't just interested in my cooking. Frank and the others were beginning to doze."

Mrs. Worth shifted in her chair, looked embarrassed, and actually started to blush. I was surprised and fascinated.

"Jesse was very handsome and he knew it. He had a little boy's appeal in his eyes. I tried to remember that he was a vicious killer, but somehow that made him more attractive.

"Carl and the others came in and I started serving breakfast. I was especially generous to Cole and Bob because their brother John had been shot and killed a few months earlier. I was very careful not to touch Jesse. Carl had told me how unpredictable and violent Jesse could be and I was afraid of what might happen.

"After breakfast they all washed at our pump, after making sure no one was around. Frank and Jessie slept in our bed and the others slept on the floor in the parlor. When they got up in the afternoon I kept busy outside with the chickens until time to get supper. Frank helped me get supper on the table. As soon as it was dark they saddled up and rode off. I saw Jesse give Carl some money."

Mrs. Wirth handed me the last cookie.

"Well, I'll tell you, Billy, I was in a terrible fix. I loved Carl, but I was mighty attracted to Jesse. I couldn't get him out of my mind, day or night. Especially night, if you know what I mean."

The cookie plate was empty. I had eaten them all. Mrs. Wirth got some more and refilled my milk glass.

They came back the next February. As soon as Jesse sat down he started crying. Between sobs he told us that the Pinkerton men had firebombed his mother's house where he and Frank were sleeping. He and Frank got away but his mother's arm was blown off. The worst thing was that his nine-year-old brother, Archie, was killed. Both Jesse and Frank really loved Archie who was retarded and I think deaf and dumb. Frank and Jesse had protected him all his life.

"I wanted so much to go put my arms around him. But I was afraid. Besides I was six months pregnant. I got busy making breakfast, but this time he didn't look at me in the old way. I was so afraid of my own feelings for Jesse that I either stayed outside or right beside Carl.

"Well, Billy, they came several times, always near morning while it was still dark. I don't remember much about those visits. I guess the next time I really remember was when Jesse and Frank came to see us with their brides. Frank had married a sweet young girl named Annie. Jesse had married Zerelda, his cousin. She was very plain and didn't have much personality, but maybe I am prejudiced. I guess I was in love with Jesse, and I suppose I still am. Every time he came I would see him occasionally look at me, with that look of longing, like he had that first day by the stove. But I swear to you, Billy, I never touched him."

"Jesse only came to see us once after that, all by himself. This was after Cole and Bob were shot and captured in Minnesota. He wanted to tell Carl about it and that it wasn't his fault. He swore that he was finished with robbing. But he wasn't. He winked at me when he left, but I don't think he meant it. I was very pregnant with my third child. After Bob Ford killed him they wrote a song about him. I loved that song and used to sing it all the time—when Carl wasn't around. Do you want to hear it?"

I said "Sure," so she sang this song in a surprisingly strong and loving voice.

> Jesse James was a lad that killed many a man,
> He robbed the Glendale train;
> But that dirty little coward that shot Mister Howard
> Has laid poor Jesse in his grave.
>
> Poor Jesse had a wife to mourn for his life,
> Three children they were brave.
> But that dirty little coward that shot Mister Howard
> Has laid poor Jesse in his grave.
>
> It was Robert Ford, that dirty little coward,
> I wonder how does he feel?
> For he ate of Jesse's bread and he slept in Jesse's bed,
> Then laid poor Jesse in his grave.

At this point Mrs. Wirth was crying and she stopped with her cheeks wet with tears. My cheeks were wet with tears too, but I was late for supper. I thanked her profusely and hurried home.

A few weeks after this, Mrs. Wirth had a stroke and her children came to take care of her. They put her bed in the front parlor. When I came in, her beautiful blue eyes were no longer dancing. Her speech was hard to understand. As soon as I sat down by her bed she said, "Billy, there is something I want to give you. Upstairs, in my top dresser drawer, there is a Blue Willow cup. Would you get that for me?"

I brought the cup down. She said, "This is the cup that Jessie drank from that first day. His lips touched this cup. No other lips but mine have touched this cup since then. My lips have touched it often."

When I came back a few days later Mrs. Wirth was much weaker. Her beautiful blue eyes were sunken. She could barely speak, but she whispered "Billy, don't ever tell anyone the stories I told you about me and Jesse James. I would be so ashamed." I promised.

And I haven't.

Until now.

(This story is true. It occurred in 1940, when the author was thirteen, in the little town of Weir, Kansas, a town near the Kansas–Missouri border.)

MY LOVE AFFAIR WITH WEE BONNIE BAKER
Bill Howland

In the summer of 1943 I was in love with Wee Bonnie Baker. I was 15 years old but had graduated from high school because of pushing by my aggressive father. We had moved temporarily to Kansas City because there were lots of well paying jobs. I was a stock boy for International Harvester. During wartime they desperately needed employees, so when I lied about my age no one questioned it.

I changed trolleys at Twelfth and Central, which was the location of the Folly Theater, the famous Burlesque House of Kansas City. My mother and father didn't get home from work until six and I got off at four so I had time to kill.

On my way home the first day of work, I noticed the poster at the front of the theater announcing "Wee Bonnie Baker." I knew who she was and was a great admirer from listening to the Lucky Strike cigarettes "Your Hit Parade" on Saturday nights. Unfortunately, my father insisted on listening to "The Grand Old Opry" on Saturday nights when I wanted to listen to the Hit Parade. Our small town druggist caught me trying to steal a small portable radio from his store, and I was so shamed by him that I never stole anything again.

I didn't know the orchestra she was with, but it wasn't Orrin Tucker's, who she sang with on the Hit Parade. He had a wonderful orchestra, and a male group called The Bodyguards backed Bonnie. They were called this to give the impression that Bonnie was so tiny and childlike that she needed protection. When Bonnie was voted the most popular singer on college campuses, I read in the paper that she was born in 1918, so at this time, 1943, she was 25. Her voice was described as "shy." But that was absolutely wrong. Bonne's voice was **SEXY**. Her biggest hit and the song she sang most frequently on the Hit Parade was a World War I song, "Oh, Johnny." As I stood there on the street corner in front of the Burlesque House I could hear in my head her voice singing every word.

> Oh, Johnny! Oh, Johnny!
> How you can love!
> Oh, Johnny! Oh, Johnny!
> Heavens above!
> You make my sad heart jump with joy,
> And when you're near I just

Can't sit still a minute.
I'm so, Oh, Johnny! Oh, Johnny!
Please tell me dear
What makes me love you so?
You're not handsome, it's true,
But when I look at you,
I just, Oh, Johnny!
Oh, Johnny! Oh!

The way she sang this song was definitely pornographic, but childishly innocent.

Every cent I earned was turned over to my father to be saved for college. I was given fifty cents each morning. The trolley cost ten cents each way, including transfers. The remaining thirty cents was for soda or candy to supplement my meager sack lunch. By going without these luxuries for the next two days I could pay the matinee charge of fifty cents.

In 1943 there was no age requirement to go to the burlesque. This was a large theater, usually sparsely populated by old men with newspapers on their laps. In spite of my teenage heightened sexuality I thought the strip teasers were not interesting. From my front row seat I could see they were old enough to be my mother, maybe even my grandmother. Their costumes were dirty and they didn't seem happy. The comedians told really stupid jokes. Then the curtains parted and there stood Wee Bonnie Baker with a microphone in front of her and a band behind her.

Bonnie Baker really was "wee." She must have been less than five feet tall. This was emphasized by her dress, which was a bright gingham check blouse and a striped short skirt, appropriate for a young schoolgirl. Her hair was brown, long and very curly. She wore a minimum of makeup. Although I knew she was twenty-five, she didn't look a day over fifteen–my age.

She sang with great intensity in that little girl voice. She sang several songs, including one of my favorites, "Billy," which was my name. I knew it was foolish, but I thought that she must have seen me in the audience and was singing to me. Of course her closing song was "Oh, Johnnie." At the completion of her performance I had to leave to get home before my parents. I was very embarrassed that everyone could see my sexual arousal.

Apparently Bonnie had a long engagement at the Burlesque House because all that summer I came to see and hear her at least twice a week. She came on promptly at 5:00. When we stock boys weren't finished filling orders, we were asked to work overtime. I refused on days I had the money for admission, saying I had a doctor's appointment.

I always sat on the first row. At least once in every session she looked directly at me and smiled. I was sure she could see the love in my eyes. I was never disappointed with her performance, and always looked forward to seeing what clothes she would be wearing that day. Once I worked up my courage and tried to go backstage. They absolutely would not let me. I was sort of relieved. I didn't know what to say. I couldn't just tell her I loved her.

At the end of summer my mother, father, and I had to leave. My father had been hired as school principal in a nearby small town and had to get things ready for school opening. I didn't want to leave, but certainly could not tell my parents it was because I went to the burlesque and was in love with Wee Bonnie Baker.

College girls didn't compare to Wee Bonnie Baker, but I gradually forgot about her until one day I read in a magazine that shortly after our one-sided love affair she gave up singing and was a telephone operator in her small Texas hometown. I was sad and disappointed. I knew she was uniquely wonderful.

Now Wee Bonnie Baker is forgotten. I was sure nobody loved her as much as I did.

One: **THE LADY AND THE *TAIGA***
Notes from a Peripatetic Professor

Audrey Lavin

The first time I taught at a university in Vladivostok, Russia, (and how many people can say that?) was in the spring of 1994. My business consultant husband and I lived in Sedunka, a village—of sorts.

Known throughout Russia as "the wild, wild East," Vladivostok and environs, which include Sedunka, were far from being tourist centers. One section of Vladivostok was still made up of log cabins, exactly as seen in pictures of the American frontier. But Vlad also had bars, restaurants, and shops.

Sedunka had none of these amenities. Houses there were set at irregular intervals along dirt roads with large puddles in front of them, even when there had been no rain for weeks. The roads met at the town "square," actually a large dirt area of a shape unknown to geometry. However, householders had been industrious. Next to each house was a stolen aluminum cargo-carrier, well disguised by dents and encrustations of debris from the roads. These metal shacks served as the contemporary equivalents of root cellars. The whole collection of dwellings and out-shacks was haphazardly set at the edge of a lovely *taiga* or birch forest.

I took a daily walk in this forest, tentatively exploring the outskirts at first, but gradually going deeper into the woods. Not knowing how large the forest was and being timid by nature, each day I ventured only several feet more into the darkness and solitude.

Solitude didn't exist in the village. When I wandered over the dirt-hardened paths, I constantly met my fellow villagers. We would exchange *dobre utras*. If asked a question, I would reply by shrugging my shoulders or pointing in some vague direction. Occasionally a *sosedka* or neighbor would walk along with me, talking constantly and not waiting for a reply, which was a good thing. Before leaving I would repeat back a few of the words he had said, closing with a cheerful *dosvidaniya*. It seemed to work. I even had one friend in the village. She knew a few words in English as I did in Russian. You didn't need much of a vocabulary to enjoy the things we did together. Larissa taught me how to make Russian cookies and how to hitchhike, Russian style–hand down, not up.

When I wasn't with Larissa or teaching at the Far Eastern State University (FESU), I enjoyed meeting and walking with my more casual *tovarisches*. Even without a common language, we could, at times, build relationships of solidarity. Sometimes we would stand in line together to make a purchase. We seldom knew what we were standing in line for. We did know that if we left our place in line to find out what was being sold from the backs of the truck somewhere in front of us, we would have to go back to the end of the line and miss the chance to buy whatever it was. Usually the wares consisted of a few toothbrushes, a dried fish, and occasionally a solitary shoe.

But in the forest, I saw no one.

I loved my solitary walks. Other living things had been in the woods before me. I could follow their paths. But all I could see were lovely straight dappled birches. Occasionally the early spring sun came through leaves, marking paths in a corresponding dappled pattern. I never saw another *comrade* or animal.

One day at a faculty meeting at FESU, I told some of my English-speaking colleagues about my daily outings.

"Audrey," Olga, the chair of the English Language Department gasped, "Two years ago, four Siberian tigers were shot and killed in that very same forest."

I gasped back at her and stumbled to a chair.

Hoping to keep me from fainting or having a heart attack, she was quick to reassure me: "Don't worry, Audrey. Please, don't worry.

"The tigers come down to the village only when they're hungry."

Two: **A JAPANESE SHAGGY DOG STORY**
Notes from a Peripatetic Professor, con't.

Audrey Lavin

In the years preceding what is probably the most horrible trifecta of disasters the world has known, scholars could concentrate on minor differences between Japanese and United States cultures.

Though during that period, academic studies of U.S.-Japanese relations examined the aggression sometimes found in Japan's history, politics, economics, and automotive competition, the studies fell short when they failed to examine popular texts used to teach English.

Some of these school books are rife with unexplored areas of hostility to U. S. values and much that we as clean, decent, dog-loving people stand for. Perhaps the texts are following the anti-canine tradition noted by Orientalist and author William Elliot Griffis when in 1882 he wrote, "In Japan, dogs are held in very little honor except the 'chin' or Japanese spaniel." Earlier, Scots naturalist Robert Fortune had written of dogs in Japan, "It was not unusual to meet with wretched specimens in a half-starved condition and covered with loathsome disease."

Today's Japanese leaders who first studied English at Japanese schools in the 80s and 90s have potentially been indoctrinated with hate and fear of the best-friend relationships cherished by Americans. Examples abound. Here is one from *Modern English: An Oral Approach-Book 7*:

Jill has three dogs on her hands.
Jack was really mad when he saw the dogs.
Both the cocker spaniel and the Dalmatian bit Jack.
Maybe Jack smells funny or something.

Ten other multiple references to people being bitten by dogs or strongly disliking them can be found in this 138-page textbook, which asks students to repeat practice sentences such as, "I can't stand dogs" and "Jack threatened the dog." Even the fictive teacher demonstrates an anti-canine bias in her textual conversational gambits that usually combine grammar lessons with pedagogical advice, such as, "You'll never learn English if you don't practice." She follows her sentence, "They'd better get tickets now or they'll miss the concert," with the sudden and uncalled for outburst, "I'll kill that dog if you don't get it out of here."

What is the effect of this indoctrination? And does *Modern English* intentionally foster aggression toward only Western breeds such as the cocker spaniels and Dalmatians mentioned in the text?

In the past, proofs could be found for such an anti-Western prejudice. Even though pre-the recent disaster, Japan had been one of the largest trading partners of the U.S., the Japanese consumer has been traditionally resistant to certain U.S. products. Maybe dogs fit under this rubric of imports.

We know that all dogs are not equal; the six related breeds of the Japanese dog, Nihon Ken, (Shiba Inu, Shikoku Inu, Kishu Inu, Kai Inu, Hokkai Do Inu, and Akita Inu) have been named National Treasures and Cultural Monuments of Japan.

Perhaps the Japanese had something on us. Certainly the Japanese dog could beat its American counterpart in a race. Step on its tail, and the result would be immediate, uncontrollable acceleration.

Three: **WHAT IF THEY GAVE A WAR AND NO ONE CAME?**

Notes from a Peripatetic Professor, con't.

Audrey Lavin

The 2009 conflict between South Ossetia and Georgia is not the first time entities of the former Soviet Union have displayed intense feelings for and against Mother Russia; it was just one of the most recent.

Thirteen years ago when the non-profit Volunteers in Overseas Cooperative Assistance (VOCA) sent my consultant husband to Chisinau, Moldova, I accompanied him. I had secured a position as Visiting Professor with the Free International University of Moldova (ULIM). Founded in 1992, the new *universitatea* had quickly earned accreditation. By the time we arrived in 1995, it boasted excellent faculty and students, not surprising in a country with a 100% literacy rating. I could conduct classes in that ever-popular foreign language, English, similar to some I had taught in the United States. Subjects included faculty seminars on teaching composition and courses for about fifty senior students in international business communication.

Lying between Romania and the Ukraine, the Moldovian Republic was the smallest country formed from the break-up of the former Soviet Union. Its citizens were as proud of its ancient roots as they were of its new found independence. When we first arrived, a national vote was taken to discard the last vestiges of the Soviet empire by making Moldova's official language Romanian instead of Russian. This did not stop Ana, the chair of the foreign language department at ULIM. She continued to heartily address me and all her other colleagues as "comrade." Habits die hard: Program notes for the opera were still in Russian, as were the voice-overs for imported films.

Aside from this subtle, though visible, dissent to the new language law, Chisinau, the capital, was a quiet, extremely friendly town. Poverty was evident. The average wage was $30 per month, compared to $90 per month in near-by Romania. No working Moldovan could afford to stay at Hotel Dacia where our apartment, courtesy of my husband's company, cost $110 a day, including the breakfast buffet.

That breakfast buffet reflected the economic condition of the country. The first few days the hotel offered a typical mid-European breakfast: hard boiled eggs, vegetables, cheeses, cereals, breads, yoghurts. But the buffet was never replenished. As hotel guests finished the eggs, then the vegetables, then the cheeses, the morning selection became smaller and smaller. By the third week, we had our choice of Corn Flakes or Rice Krispies, and that was that.

The Dacia was, at the time, the second finest hotel in Chisinau. The best hotel, we were told, was reserved for the Russian Mafia. With typical self-denigrating humor, Moldovans took for granted and laughed at the strength of the Russian Mafia influence in their culture. The first restaurant that anyone took us to was called "The Grandfather," Moldovan slang for what we call "The Godfather." When I spent a business communication class period explaining to my students how to conduct an interview to clinch getting a job, they responded by taking over another class period and acting out various satirical skits showing that the essential part of the interview to get a job in Moldova was the offering of a bribe.

The light tension over language and culture were minor distractions compared to the civil strife my husband and I have witnessed in other postings. We had worked while civil wars were going on in San Salvador, the Republic of El Salvador; twice during civil wars in Bogotá, Colombia; and twice during civil wars in the south of Russia, in Novocherkaask and Rostov on the Don. We had been tourists in Peru when the Shining Path (*sendero luminoso*) was trying to take over. We learned to keep alert when we traveled.

And we worked hard. But in keeping with the leisurely European pace of life, we had three holiday extended weekends during our first three weeks in Chisinau. By the third weekend of total immersion in Moldovan sight-seeing, we had visited most of the tourist spots in this country with a population of 4.5 million. We decided to see more of middle Europe and take a trip to nearby Odessa, Ukraine. We hitched a ride with Sergíu, a new friend who was going to see his girl-friend in Odessa, checked out of our Chisinau hotel, and started on our three-day vacation. We traveled a short time to the northeast where we were stopped at a border crossing.

A border crossing in the middle of Moldova? Not only a crossing, but one we were not allowed to go past. We were told (in not the friendliest of terms) that we were trying to enter a break away-from-Moldova republic, one that was whole-heartedly supported by Russia and, we noted, by menacing Russian troops.

Transdniestria, a very small district of Moldova, which itself is about half the size of Ohio, had declared itself independent. As proof of its independence, Transdniestria, population about 500,000, flew its own flag (usually shown without sickle and hammer), had its own national anthem, unsuccessfully coined its own money, used the Russian language, and was patrolled by heavily armed Russian troops.

But Moldova did not recognize Transdniestria as a separate state and, more insulting, did not recognize the war. The Pridnestrovian Moldovian Republic viewed the then three-year old civil war as an "incident," an internal dispute with its ethnic Russian and Ukrainian citizens.

Seemingly no one had mentioned this to the good citizens of Transdniestria or their formidable Russian allies who zealously guarded the border. As a result, we had to back away, leave the area, and find another more hospitable border crossing. In fact, in order to follow the route we had so carefully mapped to Odessa, we were forced to halt and be examined by seriously unsmiling soldiers at five border stops between Transdniestria and Moldova.

Was I frightened? Not exactly, but on our return trip to Chisinau from Odessa, we said *la revedere* to Sergíu, and changed to a public bus that took an alternate way. Just in case, we made certain that the driver was armed with well-stamped official permits.

And I began to see a deeper meaning to a sign on our hotel door, "*cerem scuze pentru deranj,*" which was followed by the official translation, "we kindly ask you to excuse us in advance for anxiety."

Fiction

VULCAN GOES ON STRIKE

A.D. Adams

Vulcan was in the volcano he used as a forge, beating one of Zeus' lightning bolts into shape. The tip shattered and one of the shards struck his cheek. It stung slightly but after making these tools for centuries, it no longer bothered him much. He dropped his great sledgehammer, causing a minor earthquake. He was getting tired of this work and limped over to his large, metal worktable and sat down. He limped because his mother Hera had thrown him off Mount Olympus. She had given birth to him, to get back at Zeus, for producing a child with another female. After she saw how ugly he was at birth, she hurled the tiny baby off the mount in anger and disgust. When he landed on a beach, the impact broke his leg. He was lucky that the sea-goddess Thetis found and raised him, even though he was crippled.

He sat on his chair rubbing his leg. It was still painful after all those centuries. He looked up and saw Apollo riding his fiery sun chariot across the sky; he had created the chariot but as usual no one had appreciated his efforts. Vulcan began to wonder why he had to live and work in a fire pit when the other gods lived on Mount Olympus in luxury. They only came when they needed something made or fixed. He was getting pretty sick of the whole mess.

He sat there looking at the nineteen, completed lightning bolts, the half-finished winged shoes for Mercury, and all the other things he was working on. Vulcan thought of his life and future and he made a momentous decision. He would not do any more work until he was given the same treatment the other gods received. It was only fair after all. He would demand to live on Olympus, be allowed to bathe in gentle waterfalls, and smell the sweet aromas of the mount. He hobbled to his bed and dropped into it, falling asleep instantly. He was awakened by a thunderous demand from Zeus.

"Where are my bolts?" the disembodied voice demanded.

"Make them yourself," he bellowed back.

"What?"

"Make them yourself," he repeated.

"That's what you do."

"Not anymore."

"What do you mean, not anymore?"

"I'm tired of living like this. I want to live on Olympus. I want what all of you have."

Zeus suddenly appeared in all his grandeur. Dressed in a sparkling white robe, his long flowing white beard and hair blew in an unfelt wind.

"Why are you not working?" he thundered.

"I quit! Find someone else to live in this pit."

"Get back to work or I will smite you down."

"Oh, go sit on the pointy end of a mountain."

Zeus reached down and took one of the completed bolts and threw it at Vulcan. It struck him in the center of his chest and exploded in a shower of sparkling crystals. As the cascade of lights cleared, there sat Vulcan laughing at Zeus.

"You think those things can hurt me? My skin has been seared so tough that nothing can harm me."

Zeus just stood there amazed Vulcan was still alive. His bolts could kill gods but Vulcan was unharmed by it. He wasn't sure what to do. Then Vulcan got up and walked to a shelf. He gathered up his tools and some clothes from a hook and put them on a large, metal plate. He folded the ends of the plate up to form a pouch and squeezed them together. He threw it over his back with one hand. He looked at Zeus with disgust and walked to the edge of the volcano and jumped. Zeus just watched powerless to stop him.

He landed in the ocean, about a hundred leagues from a small group of tropical isles. He sank to the bottom and began to walk to the nearest of the isles. Poseidon soon found out from the sea life that some big creature had fallen from the sky and was now moving through the waters of the warm, middle sea. Although old, Poseidon swam with incredible agility and speed to the location. An armada of fish, whales and dolphins led him. As he approached, Poseidon could see it was Vulcan walking along the sea floor.

"Vulcan, what are you doing here?" he asked, as he got closer.

"Taking some time off."

"Time off! What do you mean?" Poseidon asked, bewildered. Gods didn't take time off.

"I'm tired of killing myself in that pit. So I'm going to the chain of little isles just west of here and get some rest. Do you have any problems with my plans?" Vulcan completed his words in a challenging tone.

"No, you're welcome to stay as long as you wish."

"Thanks!"

Vulcan emerged from the water on a beautiful, tropical isle and lay on the warm sand, allowing the sun to dry his body. He then built a lean-to and a bed of palm fronds. He slept well in the cool night air and bathed in the warm sea each day. The warm sand and sun eased the aches of his muscles, especially his leg. The salt water of the sea seemed to even soften his heat hardened skin.

On Mount Olympus, Zeus was stomping back and forth in front of his throne. He was snarling every curse he could think of when Hera approached.

"What's wrong husband?"

"It's that damn Vulcan. He demanded to live on Olympus and when I said no, he just got up and left."

"Didn't you threaten him with one of your bolts?"

"I hit him in the chest with one. It exploded and he just laughed at me. It was like throwing a feather at a rock. All those years down in the volcano has made his skin as thick as my arm and as tough as the metal he pounds."

"I told you not to trust him. Remember how he got back up here. He trapped me in that golden throne and made me accept him as my son."

"Yeah, yeah."

"What are you going to do?"

"I'll get Mars into volcano. He's big; he should be able to handle the job. Anyway there aren't any wars right now, so Mars won't be busy."

Mars walked up to the big anvil and tried to pick up the sledge-hammer lying on the floor. He could barely get the handle up, let alone get the head off the floor. So he left it there and got a smaller hammer. He saw an unfinished bolt in a basket, next to the anvil. He picked it up with some tongs and put it on the hard surface. He lifted the hammer and struck it with all his strength and the bolt shattered into a thousand pieces. One piece went through his thigh and another grazed his side.

After the debacle with Mars, Zeus decided he needed a stronger god to handle the forge. He sent Hercules in to take over. Hercules was as dumb as a post, but Zeus figured anyone could handle some simple jobs. Apollo's sun chariot needed the wheels greased. He certainly could handle something so simple. Within minutes a wheel was crushed and the axel was broken. Apollo had to drag the chariot across the sky with a rope tied to the harness of the winded horse Pegasus. He could not control the horse or the chariot very well and it wavered all over the sky and scared the Hades out of the people below.

The device that made and stored ambrosia broke down. The great pipe, which took Mount Olympus' waste to, the core, of the world cracked and then clogged. Olympus began to smell a bit ripe and the gods were beginning to complain. Even Hera began to nag Zeus. He finally had enough and swallowed his mountain-size ego. He looked down and saw Vulcan sleeping on a beach, of a small isle. Zeus appeared in front of the sleeping figure and just stared at him.

"What do you want?" Vulcan, with his eyes closed, asked the floating form.

"I want you to come back."

"You're in my sun."

"Listen, I'll give you what ever you want."

"OK, I want that spot between Apollo and Mercury for my palace. I'm only going to work half the day, the rest of my time, I'll do as I please. I don't want to hear you bellowing at the top of your lungs whenever you want something. You will ask nicely. The rest of the stuff is on this list." Vulcan pulled a scroll out from under him and tossed it towards Zeus.

"When will you be back?"

"Later today. What happened to the sun chariot?"

"Hercules tried to fix it."

"That moron broke it, didn't he?"

"Yes." Zeus said with his head hung down.

Vulcan packed up and went back to his volcano forge. It took him three days to fix everything. He decided to start on his new palace. He made a big mold of the palace, set it in place and poured molten rock from the forge into it. All the palaces on Olympus were white except Vulcan's. It was the gray of congealed lava and more elaborate than even Zeus and Hera's palace.

Hera stood on her balcony, which overlooked all of Olympus and saw the gray, hideous thing Vulcan had built. Her anger exploded when she saw a relief on the side, of one wall. It was a woman throwing a baby off a mountain. When Zeus walked out and saw it, he laughed. The mount rumbled as Zeus' palace echoed with the screams of an angry woman.

EXCERPTED FROM PRINCE ZACHARY
Gregory E. Butler

For: The Real Prince Zachary

I

A long time ago in a forest far, far away lived a good and mighty Prince named Prince Zachary. He had many, many friends and many, many adventures and this is just one of them.

On this particular morning Prince Zachary woke up in his home in the great oak tree and came downstairs to have breakfast with Mrs. Porcupine. Prince Zachary always looked forward to breakfast. He would have the same thing every morning, his favorite berries in cream with nuts.

As Prince Zachary came downstairs and looked at the table where his breakfast normally was left, he called "Mrs. Porcupine, where're my berries and nuts?"

"Where I always put them, on the table" said Mrs. Porcupine.

"On the table? I don't see them anywhere."

Mrs. Porcupine walked out from in the kitchen, "I put them right there on the table, right where I always put them...what, they're gone!" Mrs. Porcupine walked around the table. "Look over there Prince Zachary"

Prince Zachary turned and looked and, yes indeed, there was a trail of berries and nuts leading out the front door.

"Who would come into my house and take my berries and nuts?"

"I don't know" said Mrs. Porcupine, "they must have come in while I was cleaning the dishes". Mrs. Porcupine was silent for a moment.

"What's wrong Mrs. Porcupine? You have such a strange look on your face".

"I was just thinking...whoever came in would have to have been very quiet. They would have had to open that big front door, come into the kitchen, take your berries and nuts, and leave without me hearing a thing...I just find it very strange that I didn't hear a thing."

"This is quite the mystery" said Prince Zachary.

Prince Zachary turned and quickly ran up the stairs to his bedroom on the top floor of the giant oak tree. When he got to his room he quickly changed into a shirt, pants, and shoes, grabbed his sword and ran down stairs.

"Mrs. Porcupine, I'm going to find out who came into my house and stole my berries and nuts," and out the door Prince Zachary went without another word.

II

As Prince Zachary was walking along, stopping every now and then to check the trail of berries and nuts, he noticed that the trail went past Rabbit's hole. He decided to stop and see if Rabbit was home, and if Rabbit would like to join him.

"RABBIT ARE YOU HOME?" Prince Zachary yelled down into Rabbit's hole. No answer..."HELLO....HELLO...RABBIT ARE YOU HOME?"

"Who is it?" came a voice from deep in the hole.

"It's me Prince Zachary...can you come up here please?" Rabbit's head suddenly popped out of his hole.

"Why, hello Prince Zachary, what brings you around so early in the morning?"

"Someone came into my house and stole my breakfast of berries and nuts....and the trail leads past your hole. I was wondering if you would like to come along with me?"

"Sure...sure I would," said Rabbit, "As a matter of fact I was getting ready to come over to your great tree."

"Why were you going to come over to my house?" asked Prince Zachary.

"Because I put my breakfast out this morning, I then went to my bedroom and when I came back my breakfast was gone too."

"Yours and mine!" Prince Zachary said with shock. "Well then let's get going and find out who had taken both out breakfasts and why?"

Prince Zachary and Rabbit set out to follow the trail of berries and nuts to where ever it would lead.

III

Just a few minuets later the trail of berries and nuts lead past Squirrel's tree.

"Do you think we should get Squirrel?" asked Rabbit "you know how he can be".

"Oh Rabbit you need to take it easy on Squirrel....and yes, I think we should ask him to come along". Prince Zachary and Rabbit walked up to Squirrel's tree, and Prince Zachary called up to Squirrel.

"SQUIRREL.....SQUIRREL.....ARE YOU UP THERE?" The two friends waited for a moment to see if Squirrel would answer. Just as Prince Zachary was going to call again..."yes...yes who is it...who is it?"

Squirrel called down. "It's me, Prince Zachary and Rabbit". Squirrel came out of the hole in his tree and out onto a branch and looked down.

"Why hello...hello, Prince Zachary and Rabbit, hello."

"Hello squirrel" said Prince Zachary.

"Squirrel" said Rabbit.

"Squirrel, Rabbit and I are looking for our breakfasts."

"What do you mean...looking for your breakfast?" asked Squirrel.

"Someone came into our houses and took our breakfasts. Rabbit and I have been following a trail..."

"And the trail leads past your tree" finished Rabbit.

"And we thought you would like to come along with us," said Prince Zachary.

"But if you can't we would understand," said Rabbit.

Prince Zachary turned and gave Rabbit a cross look, "What?...what did I say?" said Rabbit shrugging looking at Prince Zachary.

"Well....well I don't know...I don't know," said Squirrel as he ran back and forth on his the tree branch. "I was going to have my breakfast.....I put it out...put it out...and I don't know..."

"Calm down, just calm down Squirrel," said Prince Zachary. "Just stop pacing back and forth and tell us what is going on."

"Yes, what is going on, you nut" said Rabbit.

Squirrel stopped and looked at Rabbit, "I'm not a nut."

"Well you sure act like one, running around up there chattering a mile a minute."

"You two stop it," said Prince Zachary. "Now Squirrel, please tell me what happened."

Squirrel calmed down, and told Prince Zachary and Rabbit that early that morning he had gotten out his breakfast of acorns. He then had left the kitchen to get something and when he came back his acorns were gone. He was now very upset that he would have to go the day without his breakfast of acorns.

"Boy, everyone today is having their breakfast stolen," said Prince Zachary.

"Who would want to take our breakfast, and why?" asked Rabbit.

"That is what we will find out Squirrel, why don't you join us?" asked

Prince Zachary. "You, Rabbit, and I will go and find who has taken our breakfast, and why"

It was decided, and the three friends set off to follow the trail as it led deeper and deeper into the Great Forest.

TO BE CONTINUED...

DEARC FEARNA[1]

Marie T. Cox

"Rith! Rith!" [2]

The order to run came from my father Orthanach, our village leader and primary builder of our entrances to the hillside caves where we hid on occasions such as this.

My mother immediately dropped her work and grabbed my youngest brother Cadhla. She herded the rest of us out the door, and without a backward glance directed us to the cave not far from our village. Others from our village were fleeing to safety as well. Terrified faces reflected the panic and horror of what was to come. The Barbarians were back. My friend little Almaith fearfully glanced my way as we tried not to trip over the rocks leading toward the hill we called Dearc Fearna.

This was my second trip to that dark, dark cave; that was the last time I ever saw my beloved older sister Mor and my gentle uncle Senan. Afterwards Mother cried for days and days, moaning about "a chailin mo chroi" being "fuadaithe." Her darling girl was gone, gone forever. That day had dawned bright with promise; Mor, the prettiest of us all, hummed happily to herself as we prepared our family feast celebrating our uncle's new son Eoin. What a happy day! Eoin lived beyond the three month waiting period, the one which Senan's first three sons did not see. On that day, I had even taken a bath in honor of the occasion.

But then the day was brutally shattered by my father's loud and persistent cry to run, to run to the caves once again. My heart beat so fast that I thought I might die right then and there. And that I would be lucky to do just that. Tales of these raiders filled many of my nights with horrible images of horned men with eyes on fire. Everyone knew what they did to the captured women and young girls, even before they took them away to their ships. Oh, how these thoughts spurred my short legs! Rith, Uallach, rith!

After what seemed like an eternity, we reached the hill entrance, with me trailing a bit behind! The others had to bend very low and squeeze into the cave. Father did not want too wide of an entrance for those not wanted. Slowly we all proceeded through the tight,

---

1   Cave of the Alders, now known as Dunmore Cave near Kilkenny, Ireland

2   Run! [Irish Gaelic]

dark entrance. My short stature actually proved an asset for the second time in my life. Without the aid of any light, we headed left, to the well we knew was there. Father had drilled the village several times so that we knew our way without any aid. How I prayed for his safety now. The men had stayed behind, as always, to defend our village and elders too weak to flee; this would also delay the barbarians from pursuing us before we reached safety.

Father, please, please be safe, I prayed as we slipped and slid our way further into the darkness of the cave. Once at the entrance, I had latched on to Mother, fearful of losing her among the others. Finally, we all sat down to await what was to come next. The younger children were quietly whimpering, being shushed by their older siblings and mothers. They did not want the noise to carry outward to the entrance.

Poor gentle Ita, whose mother had been taken in the last raid; I could hear her soft prayers in the dark. Her elder sister and her husband had taken her in, and Conandil was with her now, urging her to be quiet.

Mother was rocking baby Cadhla in her arms as I tightly clung to her skirts.

Echoes of what appeared to be screams made their way to our hiding place. But who was screaming? Were our fathers and brothers and uncles victorious? Or did they lay slaughtered on our fields? Or, worse still, were they being taken off to the barbarians' lands?

In the cave, the drip, drip, drip, from the ugly cones continued as I strained to hear more from our world above. Drip, drip, drip. Nothing from outside. I heard nothing. How can that be? Have the barbarians fled?

The others must have noticed too because it was eerily silent, except of course for the dripping noise.

Then we heard what we had dreaded. Not the triumphant voices of our beloved ones but the vulgar and hoarse cries of the horned ones. No! No! It can't be, not again!

Mother gripped me too her tightly and told us to be still, no matter what happened. Ita prayed again, and Conandil did not stop her. I heard Dubhchobhlaigh, our healer, begin to chant. And then I knew, this was going to be bad.

The shouts of the evil ones continued, as did our soft prayers. They could not get through the tight opening! We were safe! I could feel tears of relief flow down my face. We could just wait them out.

Just as I thought that, I smelled the smoke. What was happening?

Mother gasped and told us that they had lit fires at the entrance; they would try and smoke us out!

We all slowly got up and continued further into the cave, as far from the smoke as we could get. Maybe we would be able to find another entrance way built into the cave. Then we could escape from the smoke and the barbarians! Learo dochais! A ray of hope!

After what seemed like a long time, we stopped and sat down once again to await our fate. Still clutching Mother's skirts, I thought of Father and uncle Senan and poor little Eoin. Were they all dead? Gentle, kind Father, please be well. Never once did he mock my infirmity or treat me different from his other children. Unlike beautiful Mor, I was born with short and stumpy limbs; I could not run as fast or as gracefully as the others, nor could I lift heavy bales or help with the harvests. But Father knew I was still worthy of something; he made me exclusively in charge of the animals; somehow he knew how much I loved them all, from the lowliest chickens to our plow horses, which I had named of course: Lorcan and Ultan. I cannot bear to think of them being hurt. They've only known love and gentle care.

And funny, funny uncle Senan! Oh, how he'd roar with laughter when visiting us with his sweet wife Mugain. Poor, poor Mugain. She never recovered from Senan's loss. Was she here in the cave with us? There were so many of us, I couldn't be sure.

The smoke wasn't too bad here. But oh how hungry I am. When will they go? I want Father! Please, please…just go! I must have muttered something aloud because Mother took me into her arms with Cadhla. She rocked us both throughout the night and into the next morning.

There was no peace for us even then. More smoke and more loud, coarse shouting. But we remained safe and out of their reach. We had plenty of water to drink. But no food. No food. Most of the time we just prayed and slept, prayed and slept.

Ita was the first to go, although she had fervently prayed to Dagda[3] and the new god. Dubhchodhlaigh could do nothing, and this scared us all. What would become of us in this dark, dark place? Had Dagda and the new god forgotten us? Or forsaken us?

And still the horned ones would not leave. Were they not satisfied with the destruction of our village? The deaths of our elders? Our fathers, brothers, uncles? What more did they seek?

---

3   Celtic father-god

After a long passage of time, Mother quietly and gently laid baby Cadhla down next to her and went into a sleep from which I could not awaken her. My family....gone. Ita gone. And now Conandil could not be stirred.

And still they did not leave.

Gently positioning myself next to both Mother and little Cadhla, I put my head down to sleep.

QUARK
Daniel Gallik

Quark was smaller than two hundred of his friends. All of Sublife, Mississippi, was composed of his comrades. The village was near whatever was around. Yes, Quark was most evasive. He was only around when he was around. He piqued often, but was never violent. He was so basic that he had no size. He would say, "I am so simple. I have no structure. I cannot be shaken away from a simple atom. But believe me, I am here. And I am glad I am here. It is so peaceful because you will never see me or touch me or harm me."

"Man or whoever thinks I like traveling in threes. Man does not know that I do not travel. I stay home. There is comfort here in Sublife."

"I like electricity," spoke the simple quark. An atom was close by. He said, "I am a multiple. You are not even a one. But I will look positive on you. I believe you are the very meaning of life." The quark barked, "I am not color or flavor. I am not up or down, strange or charming. Nor am I a mirror. They say I bond with others. I know who I am. Bonding is foolish. I would rather be alone with you."

The atom knew the scientists were naming all the other subatomic items in the world. The atom did not know why one was called a meson. Another was named a baryon. Others were titled kaons and so-ons. He thought those names were rather humorous in an exploding kind of laughing way. Quark was a good name for this non-being, he thought. The atom knew that the scientists didn't understand his importance. He thought scientists were unfairly stupid for even thinking. Yet, the atom did not like the minute creature. A quark reminded him of squawking birds and their excrement, and what they did to a man's windshield. The atom thought he should be the intellectual. But deep down he knew that quarks were.

The quark spoke, "I am between either and or. I am the speck that cannot be seen between mind and body. I am the minute realm between time and space. I am as godly as God. And I am as coy as the man who walks through life and never stops.""Essence is what we are discussing," said the atom.

"The universe within the size of nothing is the topic," a quark was denying life.

The atom was red, "You are a three-sided failure in a dualistic world."

The quark interrogated, "Then does that make you a massif in response to me? Try not to compare. There are ones smaller than I. The numbers of me are infinite. It's okay that you do not know what that means."

"Yes," said the atom, "I am what I am when I am, and I am with you." The atom liked straightening things. Dusting the house. Vacuuming. And, sure, exploding at times. "I will destroy you one day, and that will be all."

The quark, "I am laughing at you, you beast! You will do everything some day. I will still remain right here. Right here beside you. Ha, ha! In the mean time, Sublife keeps breathing. We all, all are glad about that.

GUILT'S REPRISAL

Linda Toles Lasley

Sarah heard the man seated behind her on the bus say, "Pack up the kids and get out of town. I'll meet you at your mother's."

Sarah pretended to be engrossed in the newspaper she was reading while hoping to hear more of the man's conversation. All she heard was a heavy sigh as the man snapped his cell phone shut. Placing the paper on the seat beside her, she reached into her purse for her mirrored compact. Pretending to be checking out her make-up, she positioned the mirror so that she could see the man. He was staring out the window and his forehead was wrinkled in deep concentration. She quickly closed the compact as the man turned away from the window.

He leaned forward and said, "Excuse me, may I borrow your newspaper?"

"Sure," said Sarah as she handed him the paper.

Sarah wondered what could be going on in his life to cause him such concern. His hand had been trembling when he took the newspaper from her, and there were beads of perspiration on his forehead. He was definitely worried!

Fifteen minutes later, the bus came to a stop, at Emerson Street. Several passengers arose to depart, including the man seated behind her. As he was passing by, he placed the newspaper on the seat next to her and said, "Thanks."

"You're welcome," Sarah said. She smiled up at him. He quickly turned away; but not quickly enough to prevent Sarah from seeing the unshed tears in his eyes.

Before the bus had pulled away from the curb, they heard tires squealing and people shouted, "Oh no!" The bus driver turned off the engine, quickly opened the door and bounded down the steps. Sarah and the remaining passengers on the bus stood and craned their necks to see what was happening. Sarah gasped and put her hand to her mouth as she saw a man lying in the street. "It's him," she softly muttered, "the man who was sitting behind me."

The bus driver returned and said, "I'm sorry folks, but since I was an eyewitness to the accident, I have to wait and give a statement to the police. You all have to get off here. I'll radio dispatch and have them send out another bus."

"What happened?" someone asked.

"The guy just walked out into traffic and stood there," the driver replied.

When Sarah picked up the newspaper a folded piece of paper fell out. On the outside was written, "Please see that my wife gets this. Her name is Jane Thompson. She lives at 119 Park Avenue in Charlottesville. Thanks." Sarah stuffed the note in her purse and exited the bus. She went into the coffee shop up the street and ordered a cup of hot tea. Settling in a booth, she took the note out and started to read:

"My darling Jane,

Please forgive me for the hurt I know I'm causing you and the kids; but I did it to protect you.

You see, twenty years ago I worked for a big insurance company in California. I reached a point in my life where things started to really go wrong for me. I was in so much debt that I didn't see how I could ever get out from under it. One day, I discovered a way that to get the money I so desperately needed. I'm ashamed now to say that I embezzled it from the company. I left before anyone found out, changed my identity and moved to Virginia. Shortly thereafter I met you...and well you know the rest. I want you to know, Jane, that the years with you and raising our family have been the happiest years of my life. I only regret that we can't continue being together; but, I fear now that I may be putting my family in danger.

Yesterday I received an anonymous message at work which said, "Peek-a-boo, we've found you." And today when you called me and said that several threatening messages had come in at home for me, I knew that they had found me. I'm so sorry, my dear Jane, that I did this to you and the kids. At least now, with me gone, you'll be safe. Please forgive me.

All my love, Robert."

Sarah sat back. Then suddenly leaned forward again, turned the letter over and looked at the name on the outside. "Jane Thompson," she whispered. "That means this note was written by Robert Thompson." Sarah's heart began to pound. She pulled out her cell phone and called her friend, Marcia. When she answered Sarah blurted out, "Marcia you have to meet me, NOW!

"Why what's wrong?" Marcia asked.

"I can't tell you about it over the phone. Please meet me; it's urgent! I'm at the coffee shop on Emerson," she pleaded.

When Marcia arrived, Sarah went out and got into the car. She told her that she had been on the bus with Robert Thompson that morning and when he got off the bus, he had walked into the flow of traffic and killed himself.

"What," exclaimed Marcia in disbelief.

"That's not all," Sarah told her. Her hand shook as she handed Marcia the note addressed to Jane. "Read this," she said. "He left it on my seat."

When Marcia finished reading the note and looked up, Sarah said, "We caused that man to kill himself."

Marcia responded, "We had no way of knowing this would happen when we sent him that peek-a-boo message. It was just a joke."

"I know," said Sarah. "But it DID happen! Did you also make calls to his house this morning?"

"Well," Marcia said as she lowered her gaze; I thought about what a jerk he always was at work so I called his house and left a couple of messages. I wanted to shake him up a little that's all."

"Marcia!" Sarah exclaimed.

"Look," said Marcia. "I feel bad that he killed himself; but, that message and those phone calls were just to get back at him for being so mean to me at work. It's not our fault that he had a criminal past that he thought had caught up with him."

Sarah shook her head, "I don't know Marcia, I wish I could feel like you do; but, all I can think about is that someone killed himself and I may be partly responsible."

Taking the note from her, she said, "I'm going to deliver this note like he asked me too."

Marcia reached over and gently placed her hand on her friend's arm.

"Sarah, please don't say anything," she pleaded. "It'll only make things worse. We can't reverse what has been done. He was hiding from a bad past. Believe me, it would have eventually caught up with him."

"I guess you're right," said Sarah.

Marcia dropped Sarah off at Park Avenue. A few minutes later, Sarah was standing in front of the home of Jane Thompson. When she rang the doorbell, an older white haired woman answered the door.

"Jane Thompson?" Sarah asked.

"No, the lady replied. "I'm her mother. May I help you?"

Faltering for a moment, Sarah finally managed to say, "I have a note for Jane."

"I'll see that she gets it," the lady said while extending her hand for the note.

"I'd like to give it to her personally," Sarah said.

A voice from behind the lady said, "It's alright mother." Then a younger lady appeared, her eyes red and swollen from crying.

"I'm Jane Thompson," she said.

"Mrs. Thompson, my name is Sarah. I was on the bus with your husband this morning," Sarah told her.

Jane Thompson raised her hand to her throat as fresh tears filled her eyes. "Please come in," she said.

"I won't be staying," Sarah said quickly, as she stepped inside. "I just came to give you this note your husband left on the seat beside me; and, to tell you how sorry I am for your loss."

"Thank-you," Jane responded as she took the note. "Did you speak with Robert?" she asked.

"No, not really," Sarah answered. "He was sitting behind me and he asked to borrow my newspaper and he said thanks when he returned it. That's all."

"I see," said Jane. "Well, thanks for coming Sarah."

Two young children appeared and stood by their grandmother who had remained standing a little behind Jane. Sarah noticed that they too had red swollen eyes.

Looking at Jane she said, "I have to go now. Again, I'm very sorry." She quickly turned and opened the door. She wanted to get out of there before the tears she felt forming in her eyes started streaming down her face. Once outside, she let the tears flow as she walked to the bus stop. Before boarding the bus, Sarah wiped the tears from her eyes and face. When the bus stopped at University Boulevard, Sarah got off, stepped out into the street, turned to face the traffic and just stood there.

A few hours later, Sarah's parents stood beside the hospital bed, looking down at their daughter lying there in a coma. They looked up as Marcia came in.

Sarah's mom said, "They say she was trying to kill herself. That she was crying when she got off the bus; and that she purposely stood in oncoming traffic. Do you know why she would do such a thing?"

Marcia averted her eyes, shook her head and said, "Excuse me," as she fled from the room. Going into the restroom, Marcia burst into tears and cried, "Oh Sarah," over and over as the tears flowed. When she regained her composure, Marcia returned to the hospital room. Mrs. Howard, Sarah's mom, came over and put her arm around her.

"Are you alright?" she asked.

Marcia nodded then said, "Why don't the two of you go get a cup of coffee and something to eat in the cafeteria. I'll sit with Sarah. I promise to come get you if there's any change."

Mr. Howard said, "Thank you, Marcia."

Turning to his wife he said, "Come on honey, you need to eat something. Marcia will be here with Sarah."

When they had left, Marcia pulled a chair up beside Sarah's bed. As tears welled up in her eyes she said, "Sarah, I'm so sorry. I should have realized how upset you were about all of this." Her voice broke as she started to sob. "I promise you, Sarah, when you wake up, I will be here for you; and, I'll do whatever it takes to help you get through this. Please don't give up on life because of something I've done. We CAN get through this."

The door opened and Sarah's parents walked in. Mr. Howard said, "I couldn't get her to stay in the cafeteria and eat. She insisted we bring our coffee and sandwiches up here."

"I understand," said Marcia as she rose to her feet. "Please excuse me. I have to leave now; but, I'll be back later. Please call me if she wakes up."

"We will," assured Mr. Howard. "And thank you for coming Marcia."

When Marcia returned home, she was very despondent. After several hours of crying and wondering what to do, she picked up the phone and dialed.

When the voice on the other end said, "Crisis Line, how may I help you?"

Marcia took a deep breath and said, "I need to talk to someone. I inadvertently caused the death of one person and I'm also responsible for my best friend being in the hospital in a coma. Please help me. I don't want anyone else to get hurt."

THE OLD MAN OF THE LAKE
Joseph McLaughlin

As I read my poems to the old man on the other side of the camp-fire, I continued to note details of his appearance: dirty ball cap, scruffy five-day beard, thick glasses, body wrapped in an old Indian blanket. Occasionally, the breeze moved the smoke and flames in a new direction, revealing bare feet in worn-out sandals as he sat cross-legged on a log.

He merely nodded and smiled as I read. When I stopped, he seemed content, and I was a little annoyed that there wasn't more reaction to my work. I wanted his approval and endorsement, though one wondered what that would be worth, and it wasn't forthcoming. He had listened with a bemused tolerance and closed eyes, remaining silent.

Was he asleep? I stared through the fire and smoke at the top of his head and the darkness over his shoulder. He looked up and the smile had disappeared. As I gazed into his dark eyes, he seemed so familiar—I knew this man. The scary part was the feeling that he knew me as well. Finally, he spoke in a voice surprisingly whiny and southern.

"You are sometimes nine, sometimes fourteen, never older than twenty or twenty-one," he slowly drawled, and his leathery face again wrinkled into a mock smile while I puzzled over that.

"I'm forty-six years old," I quietly affirmed.

"Biological age," he snickered, poking the fire with a stick so it would flame up again instead of smoking.

Go and see the wise old man, my friends had told me. *He lives in the pine trees beside a lake winter and summer–only accepts one visitor at a time*, and I came and read to him and now he seemed to be psychoanalyzing me. Unsure what to say, I lay back upon a blanket he had given me. The fire light flickered and danced on the underside of the leaf canopy above us.

"Those are my ages," I finally admitted. "I change from moment to moment, but those are my spirit ages."

"Uh-huh," he agreed.

I rolled my head to see him through the smoke. "Who are you?" I asked.

"Who are you?" he twanged.

"How do you know so much about me?"

119

"How do you know so little about me?"

Not satisfied, he stood to poke the fire more vigorously, nearly losing the blanket in the process. His fly was either unzipped or broken, and the faded jeans had holes in the knees.

"Why can't I grow up?" I wondered after a silence.

"Maybe you're afraid of becoming like me," he replied as he sat down again on the log. I resented his comment but stopped myself with a tongue bite.

"Count to ten," he chuckled.

What?" Had he read my mind?

"Your mother told you to count to ten when you're angry, but you just rush through it. The ancient advice is to count ten breaths—quite a different matter, eh?

"Why aren't we talking about my writing here?" I demanded.

"Dunno." He stared again into the flames.

I sat up to explain my position in a logical way. "I don't want to grow up," I acknowledged. I'd always believed my naivete was a source of creativity and worked to preserve a childlike outlook on the world.

"You don't have to grow up," he intoned very slowly, apparently hoping I'd get the message and quit making a big deal of it. The implication was that the choice was mine, and I could simply possess these youthful selves, acknowledge them, celebrate them, stop comparing them to "adult" people. Then I remembered a prayer affirmation I'd used for years, one I always turned to during crises.

"I will be young in spirit forever," I recited, not even looking up for a sign of approval, realizing I had achieved my request.

"Yeah, that's it," he said after a long silence. Together we stared into the dying fire. A farm dog howled from the far side of the lake. The crickets roared. An unexpected wind moved the treetops and briefly encouraged the fire...

In the morning, I awakened to discover the old man was gone. I'd been sleeping on both our blankets on his side of the dead fire. From that day on, the woods and the lake were mine.

THE UNDISCOVERED COUNTRY
Joseph McLaughlin

I found myself in a strange place, ankle-deep in light surf on a sandy beach. The roar of the ocean and the whistling wind were disorienting, and I couldn't tell from the eerie half-light and the low, red sun whether it was morning or evening. Far out on the water, rays streamed and filtered through clouds in bursts of pink and violet. Something told me I had come from that direction, that my home was over there, far away.

The wind gusted again, and I felt a chill and realized my clothes were soaked as if I'd been immersed in the warm ocean water. I touched my head and my hair was wet. I could feel rivulets running down my back and realized even the clothes were strange–a white, oversized tee shirt and dark blue pants rolled up to the knee as if I'd planned to go wading. I kicked the water with a bare foot, making a musical splash against the deeper chorus of breaking waves and wondered how I'd gotten there. I felt surprisingly calm and peaceful as the waves broke rhythmically around me. I tried to recall my home and family and friends I'd left behind. The enemies, too. But they were all vague memories. I was too tired to concentrate very long. Had I been shipwrecked? Was I exhausted from the struggle to survive? My only sensation was one of complete and total emptiness.

"Hello!" I croaked weakly into the wind, just to see if I had a voice. I splashed some more in the refreshing water and felt a fish or crab bite my toe. "Hey!" I shouted with a laugh, getting some energy back. Then, in the midst of my childlike play, I sensed I was being watched.

I turned to see someone at the water's edge, which by then was about fifty yards behind me. The tide was coming in, and I was up to my knees in water, but I couldn't take my eyes off the girl who was standing there. Lifted by the wind, curls and sashes and streamers flowed from her long, white dress and golden hair, and I wondered if she could help me. "Hello!" I called again, and she made a slight gesture with her hand, inviting me closer.

I waded slowly toward her across the shallow surf, stopping a few paces away to study her face. It was serenely beautiful, but not sensual. The eyes were pale blue, and her smile was slight, the pink

121

lips closed indulgently, and the corners of her mouth turned up the slightest bit. If anything, she seemed to be amused by my situation.

Without a sound, the lovely creature turned and began walking slowly across the sand toward the cliff behind the beach. Was I to follow? I stood transfixed until she turned again and–with a bolder, more insistent gesture–urged me forward.

We crossed the sandy beach and came to the base of the mountain where the girl started up a narrow path hidden among shrubs and bushes. She stepped so lightly over the rocks and stones that I wondered if she weighed anything at all. Then I realized I was also barefoot and not wincing with each step.

It was a surprisingly easy climb up the zigzag path to the top of the craggy wall. Above the rocks was a gentler, grassy slope leading to a copse of dark trees. Stopping to rest for a moment on this final ledge, I turned to look again at the sea gleaming so splendidly below and the shrinking, white strip of beach. From this vantage point, one could see up and down the coast for miles.

By then the sun was fully up, turning from red to yellow, and I realized it was morning. The air was fresh and cool, and the breeze was even gustier on these heights. The blue sky hovered over the green sea like a mother, and white gulls wheeled overhead, crying in their tongue.

Then something up the coast caught my eye. At first, I thought it was a post or log, then I detected movement. Someone was standing in the surf, just as I had. Should I go back down to see? Then I remembered my guide and looked up to where she stood on the grassy hill. Would she wait for me?

As I turned back to the sea view, I noticed yet another dark spot emerge from the last reach of the surf and gradually unfold itself to stand erect, becoming a person looking about. Then another appeared, and another. Up and down the coast every few hundred yards someone was walking onto the beach to be met by one of the ethereal guides. I had only been one of many.

Amazed, I looked to my companion for an explanation, but her expression had not changed. She gestured again for me to follow, and I knew I must. At that moment, I realized I had come there to stay.

POINSETTIAS AND OTHER PROBLEMS

Eugenia A. Parrish

I can't find my arm. I know it's there, but I can't find it. I try to tell them, but my tongue isn't working today. On good days, I can talk, at least enough to say hello, ask them to lift up the bed, let them know I want more Tylenol. That's if they're listening.

Usually they're listening more to the bullying whine of the head nurse down the hall. Usually they're rushing through with the sponge, the flopping me over like a fish, the tucking sheets around my dead legs. It's hard to get their attention when they're used to old folks who let them know in a screech if there's something wrong. And they're understaffed. I hear them talking about it. Can't help it – they talk over me like it's a baby they're diapering. Yesterday one of the aides had a fever of a hundred and two and they made her come in and work a full shift. They don't care if we all catch whatever it is.

I try to tell Bill I can't find my arm. He strokes my hair with his hard old hand and asks if I want the TV on. He's been so good. It surprises me that he's in here every day. There was always so much at the house that he had to take care of. There was never time for vacations, let alone sitting in here with his wife who can't even wipe herself anymore.

Nodding my head is easy, so I do, and he turns on the TV. It's one of those crappy judge shows. I hate them, people sniveling at each other over nothing. I used to sit in the kitchen with a good book while he'd take his tray into the TV room so he wouldn't miss anything. He has such fun shaking his head over how stupid those people are. Me, I don't need stupid. Stupid is having a stroke that doesn't kill you right out.

My daughter arrives with a bunch of some kind of flowers. And another damn jigsaw puzzle. When you can't even hold a piece for yourself, what's the point. I used to like to watch her do it, watch the picture forming, colors turning into animals or houses. But Bill kept saying how boring it was. He's right, it is boring, so I wish she'd stop.

"Why aren't you at work?" I ask her, or try to. It doesn't come out very clear, but she gets it.

"It's Saturday, Mom." Lorrie doesn't say it like I'm stupid, which is nice. But there's a feeling I sometimes get, like a pat of rancid butter in my stomach. Used to be I always knew what day it was, even after I retired and it didn't matter. But then again, what's it matter now?

She puts the new flowers in the blue plastic cup that has my name stuck to it so my roommate won't use it and get my cooties. I don't know why they gave me a water glass. If I could swallow anything I wouldn't need this tube coming out of my stomach like a third arm.

Finally she turns around and sees the big poinsettia plant taking up the whole table.

"Wow, Mom. Who brought that thing in?"

The pat of rancid butter moves, sliding across my stomach.

"Your two cousins brought it," Bill snaps. He's been waiting to tell her about it all morning. He used to tell me about things that bothered him, but he's not supposed to upset me. So he tries to tell Lorrie but she won't listen. "It's nice," is all she says, and turns away.

I want to say to her, listen to him, dammit – he's talking to you. I want look out the window too, but it's hard to see anything from where I am. I'd like to see a damn tree.

He's getting wound up about the poinsettia.

"Nice! For Chrissake, look at it! Look at how big it is! You'd think they'd have more sense," He rakes the last word like a bronc-buster rakes his spurs down a horse's sides. "You can't put anything on the table with that thing sitting there."

"I think it brightens up the room," she says. "Anyway, it was nice of them."

I hate it when she's dense. He stays mad about things for days if nobody pays attention. Now he'll be as mad at her as he is at her cousins. For thirty years she can't get along with him. So she moves out of state. I don't know why she came back, she hates it here. Because of me, I guess.

A moment of silence sours the room. I want to tell someone about the rancid butter. It slides from my stomach into my guts.

He's talking through his teeth, explaining it to her like he always does, as though she's retarded.

"I brought that table in here to hold her things. I didn't carry it in to have it taken over by some stupid plant that nobody in their right mind would buy."

He's pushing her to understand, to get it. I wish he wouldn't talk through his teeth. It makes him look and sound demented. He's right, though, it is a stupidly big plant. Margaret and Em laughed when they brought it in. I laughed too. It felt good to laugh. When I laugh, the butter goes away.

I wish the plant would go away. You can hardly see the table under it, or the basket full of cards people have sent, or my exercise charts or the fresh clothes Bill sets out for later. There's even this little angel statue sent over by the nurses at the hospital after I moved here. It says I'm their angel. It's nice, but I can't remember any of them.

And there's the picture of me dancing that he brought in to show everyone how healthy I used to be. Like they care what I was before.

I've watched him arrange it all and sort it, adding and subtracting things. Finding the most efficient place for each thing, just like he does at home.

Listen to me, would you. Home. This is my home now.

"Don't you like it?" Lorrie asks me.

Oh, the plant. Why won't she listen to him? Why doesn't she just take it away? The nurses would if he asked them, but he won't. He can't ask for things, he can only get angry when you don't understand what he wants.

I say, "Too . . . big," pushing it out, a grunt for each word.

"I guess it is." She looks over at it doubtfully. "Maybe we could trim it or something."

I nod, but nobody's looking at me. Bill's gone over to the window, staring out, his jaw set, and I'm reminded of his old father. Catch that bastard spending all day at a nursing home with a sick wife. He had a mouth like a snapped-shut purse. I can see Bill's mouth doing it now, and I want to tell Lorrie to get rid of the plant.

She's dumping the new puzzle onto my wheelchair tray. It's a Thomas Kincaid, she says. I feel the tears come up and run over and down my face, I can't stop them. I have a Kincaid painting, somewhere. I'd like to have that here instead of the dancing thing.

She's seen the tears.

"What, Mom? What's wrong?"

I shake my head and wave at the puzzle with the arm that works.

"What, you don't like it?" She speaks in a cheerful way that she must've learned at that group home where she works. It's to let me know that it's okay, whatever I'm feeling. I feel tired.

I shake my head and then nod. And the frustration bites in hard and I start making small wailing sounds, I can't help it. Bill hurries over from the window, elbowing her out of the way.

"Is the puzzle too much?" he says anxiously, rubbing my arm, patting my cheek. He's so gentle it brings more tears. He pushes the puzzle pieces toward her. "You better take it away. She doesn't want it."

Lorrie starts to gather it up.

"No," I grunt.

She looks at me for a moment. I look back through the wet and see her and she sees me. It happens sometimes, just between us.

"You cry for happy?" she asks.

I nod and we laugh. It's an old joke from an old movie. Mom's crying for happy again.

She puts the pieces back on the tray. He opens his mouth, then shuts it like a purse and makes a big show of watching the TV, though I know he's not. Lorrie picks out all the flat-sided pieces and shows me how she's making the border. I watch her and wonder where my hand is.

SAD TAXI

Eugenia A. Parrish

The back seat of the taxi smelled like a cat box.

Danny asked the driver, "Do you smoke?"

"I told everybody I quit," the man said.

He'd not spoken since he picked Danny up, and now they were sitting at the curb.

"But you haven't," said Danny.

He patted the pack until a cigarette stuck out. He held the pack across the seat back. The driver took it.

"Thanks, man."

Danny heard the pop of the cigarette lighter being pushed in. How did the guy stand driving around in such a piece of crap? It had bench seats, for crying out loud, not even old-type buckets. He thought of the car that he sold when he quit college and joined the Army. Sweet ride. Wonder who had it now. Should've left it for his little brother. Joey was almost old enough to drive now.

Danny thumbed his lighter and sucked the smoke in.

The man said without turning around, "You gettin' out or what?"

"Gimme a minute."

Out in the dark his parents' house blazed like a theater. They were all waiting for him, and he could hear voices, happy and laughing. It made his stomach sick.

At his feet rested the duffel bag with his dishonorable discharge papers jammed in somewhere. If he never went in, would they find out how he'd screwed up? Of course they would. Word would get back. His father wouldS hate his guts. His mother would drive across town to shop at different stores. Maybe they'd get over it. Eventually.

And Joey? Joey might start smoking weed or popping pills or something, hanging out with the creeps at the back of the school auditorium. He was a crazy kid, tense and strung out. Always jumping at big-brother Danny, wanting high-fives. Danny could send him a letter, maybe. Tell him how he shouldn't screw up his life too. It would be easier to write it than say it, less likely he'd break down in front of the kid. But Danny suspected if he left it for a letter, it would never get done.

"Buddy." The man's voice was indifferent. "The meter's runnin'."

"Yeah, yeah." Danny sucked on the cigarette, threw it out the window. He dragged the big duffel up onto his lap and put his hand on the door handle. A huge emptiness swelled in his stomach and he wondered if he'd need to throw up.

The driver moved his head and Danny could see his eyes in the rear view mirror. Dark eyes with heavy brows.

"Some party," the man said. "Ain'tchu goin' in?"

"Maybe not."

Danny felt the man watching him. Then the front seat creaked as he shifted and laid his right arm along the ragged seat back.

"Ahh, shit, kid. Y'know, I sat outside a house once, just like this. Long time ago." The eyes glanced at him again. "Guts tied up?"

Danny let out a puff of a laugh. "Yeah."

The man nodded. "Me too. I ran up about three bucks worth just sittin' there, and that was a lotta years ago."

"Your folks?"

"Just the wife. My sumbitch boss had a bad day 'n' fired me. So I punched him and took money outen the register and blew some of it on booze. Then I took a freakin' taxi home and sat there. You b'lieve that? I didn't have enough left for her to buy groceries or pay the rent. But I had enough for a bus ticket. So I split."

"What happened to your wife?"

"Dunno. Never saw the place again. I figger she got a divorce. Best thing for her. We never woulda made it anyhow. I wasn't no good in them days. Ain't much better now, but it don't matter to nobody but me, y'know?" He turned in the seat. "You want I should take youse to the bus station?"

"You get married again?"

The man didn't answer for a moment.

"Y'know, it's funny, but I just always felt like I was still married to her."

"Maybe you should look her up. Maybe she feels the same."

After another pause the man said, "Nah. It's too late."

They sat for a moment in the sad cab. Then Danny handed the man his last twenty for a six-dollar fare. "Keep it."

He got out, shut the door and watched as the car slid away and faded into the dark. Then he took his duffel and went up the walk.

STYX AND STONES

Eugenia A. Parrish

I tried to watch the sailboat without seeming to, as soon as I spotted it slicing back through the breakwater entrance. Better not to look like I cared too much. Better not to look as if I'd spent four tedious hours drinking cappuccinos and planning what I would say to Michael, and how I would say it.

The sun was setting behind the boat. The island on the horizon was black and sharp and low, like ridgescales on the spine of a sleeping beast. The water moved darkly between it and me. I hadn't been this close to the sea in years. I might have enjoyed sitting in the café above it, if my husband had been with me instead of spending the day on the island with his friends.

The boat drifted up and bumped the dock. I put my hand up to shield my eyes and checked each silhouette, not seeing his. It was just like Michael to sulk below in the tiny cabin.

The sun had still been straight overhead when Michael and I had driven to the marina after a stiff and stilted morning. In spite of my protests, he'd driven too fast, afraid we'd keep them waiting. All the way I'd tried to talk sense to him.

"Michael, it's such a little boat."

"It's a big island."

"Surrounded by water. Lots and lots of water."

"Barbara, it's just a day-trip."

"Terrific. You want me to spend an entire day with six people ignoring me."

"They wouldn't ignore you if you'd just –"

"What?"

"Just be nice."

I rolled my eyes. "You know this is ridiculous. You'll hate it. Just tell them we have too many things to do. We can have lunch at the restaurant and go home."

I glanced sideways at him, searching for the look that told me I'd gotten through to him. It had always been there before, that sweet look of surrender. It was there when I told him we had to buy the house. Prices would go up. If we didn't buy it, someone else would, and we'd never find another like it. The look was there when I told him that the pill hadn't worked but it was alright, a baby wouldn't cost much if we cooked our meals at home and watched television instead of watching co-workers carousing at the local sports bar.

And it was there when I told him that quitting his job would put us on welfare. Hadn't he had enough of hairbrained schemes that were supposed to make us rich and never did? Did he remember it was my paycheck that had carried us for months when he was in the hospital? Well, did he?

When we arrived at the dock he held out his hand to help me into the boat, as though he hadn't heard a word I'd said. The high sun shadowed his eyes black, struck angles across his neck, and highlighted the old scars on his wrist. I jerked my hand back and he dropped his arm. But to my rage, he hadn't stepped back from the boat, he'd stepped *into* it. And he was a stiff shadow looking out at the horizon as Charlie shoved off from the dock.

I'd thought of taking the car and going back to the house. I thought of packing up the baby and going to my mother's. Then I thought of living without him. Of how life had been before I met Michael, living in apartments at the end of dark hallways where the air was thick with the smell of fried food and spilled liquor. Of being alone in the night. I sat and thought, and sat and thought.

Now I stood, brushed off my skirt and walked down to the dock. Charlie leapt out to tie the boat up. He stooped and gave each line several extra turns, yanking on them unnecessarily and ignoring me as I stepped gingerly onto the slippery planks. The other men and their wives, tired-looking and silent, came from the cabin below and unloaded coolers and towels. Little waves pushed against the underside of the dock, making it breath. Up and down, in and out. I tensed against the nausea. A scuttering breeze carried the bitter smell of day's end.

"Alright," I said to Charlie. "Where is he?"

"He's not here," said Crystal, Charlie's top-heavy wife. She brushed past me, her rope soles scritching on the dock.

"I can see that. Is he coming out? Or am I supposed to go below and get him?"

One of the other wives hefted a cooler onto her hip. "She said he's not here. He told us he was going to take a long swim on the other side of the island and he'd be taking the ferryboat home."

Through slashing shards of setting sun, I saw Charlie straighten slowly, like a cat sensing a storm that hasn't arrived yet.

"We got becalmed on the way back," he said. "The ferry passed us. Wasn't he on it?"

I hardly heard him. "Michael can't swim," I said.

130

SEANCE CHAT@LIVINGDEAD.COM
G. L. Rockey

from BATS IN THE BELFRY, BELLS IN THE ATTIC

From: Sigourney@alien.com
Ken, how did you get in the apartment?

From: Louie@down.com
AM, what are the chances or renewing membership? Let's talk.

From: Ken@bogeyman.com
Sigourney, I broke down the door.

From: Adolf@hot.com
Anybody know how to delete URL's?

From: Lola@sex.com
Anybody need a date?

From: Sigourney@alien.com
Ken, why, you had a key?

From: Joe@$$forkiss.com
Lola, I do.

From: Gertrude@stein.com
All of you, if this conversation doesn't get any better better better
fast, I'm logging off.

From: AM@up.com
AM is okey dokey.

From: Ken@bogeyman.com
Sigourney, I wanted to make a statement. Every since you brought
me home, gave me this stupid Ken name, you've been promising to
take me out to dinner.

From: Ben@franklin.com
Hey Gertrude, stick it.

From: Lola@sex.com
Joe, how much?

From: Vincent@price.com
Help, I'm trapped in an eggroll!

From: Joe@$$forkiss.com
Lola, before we talk bucks, what do you look like?

From: LarryF@hustler.com
I have a great idea for a TV sitcom, it takes place in a men's locker room with a peep hole into the lady's . . . I can't give away the plot, but it would be live from behind the scenes, three hours, prime time, anybody want to write it?

From: Bill@zsu.com
I need a synopsis (English Lit) on The Brother's Karamozzz (spelling) by that Russian guy.

From: Lola@sex.com
Joe, I have long blond hair and blue eyes, am five foot two, 22-30-40

From: Peg@bitch.com
Why couldn't it have been the Sister's Karamozzz?

From: Gertrude@stein.com
Franklin, be that way, and to all of you, I'm going no mail forever ever ever ever.

From: AM@up.com
AM is okey dokey.

From: FScott@fitz.com
Larry, what will you pay if I write it?

From: Allen@funt.com
Larry F., I think you stole my idea.
From: Kathy@bleed.com
Sigourney, why did you lock the door on Ken? And why don't you take him to dinner?

From: Pete@guy.com
Joe, re: Lola—little tits, big ass.

From: GeorgeW@mtvernon.com
Adolf, you can get a delete URL's download at http\\history.kill. dada.com for twenty me's, get it?

From: Ed@sullivan.com
Bill, I had the Flying Karamazovs Brothers on my shew, they're jugglers, hope that helps.

From: Vincent@price.com
Help, I'm trapped in a fortune cookie!

From: Rod@serling.com
Everybody is stealing my ideas!

From: LarryF@hustler.org
FScott, what do you mean, pay?

From: Anton@chekov.com
Rod/Larry, the peep hole is my idea, read my story, "On The Sea," and relax.

From: Sigourney@alien.com
Kathy, buzz off, it's none of your business.

From: Michael@wingsgolden/gate.com
Adolf, why do you want to delete your URL's?

From: Sally@less.com
Joe, I do what Lola does for free.

From: Vincent@price.com
Help, I'm trapped in a bottle of Kikkoman soy sauce!

From: Peggy@bitch.com
I still want to know why it has to be Brother's Karazozz, aaand who the hell is AM?

From: Sigourney@alien.com

Ken, I don't think I want to see you anymore

From: AM@up.com
AM is okey dokey.

From: Harry@houdini/\\/.rosabelle.com
Vincent, one, two, three and there is a way to get out. Buy handcuffs on tomorrow nights' PBS antique show. P.S. Interested to know how you got the computer in the soy sauce jar with you.

From: Ken@bogeyman.com
Sigourney, does this mean you don't love me anymore?

From: Peggy@bitch.com
Ken, awwwwwww, poor thing.

From: Bess@spousehoudini.com
Harry, where are you?

From: AM@up.com
Repeat, AM is okey dokey.

From: Sigourney@alien.com
Ken, yes and I get to keep the lap top, cell phone, and Oreck vacuum cleaner. You can have Tammi Fay, the cookies, and your rubber doll. As to you Pegs baby, get screwed.

From: Harry@Truman.com
Vincent, all you need now is a Little Boy, Enola Gay, and a Nagasaki. Hee hee hee.

From: Mao@greatwall.com
AM, are you Who from Hunan?

From: Yoko@Hiroshima.com
Harry@Truman babes, waa go 'wound come 'wound.

From: Lucy@producerhollywood.com
Bill, The Brother's Karamazov is a movie staring Bruce Willis and Danny DeVito. Bruce owns a bagel factory in Iraq funded by the CIA. Danny delivers.

From: AM@up.com
Why is everybody ignoring me?

From: Louie@down.com
Because you're dead, now shut up.

From: Peggy@bitch.com
What has no top and three bottoms? Hint, rhymes with hola and starts with L. As to you Sigourney, eat it!

From: Ernest@hem/bigfish.com
All you guys need a good shit detector. And you, Bill@zsu, the Russian guy is Fedor Dostoevski. The story is The Brother's Karamazov. In a nutshell it's about God being dead and, if He is, everything is history so you can go pig out and muck anybody who gets in your way. That's free. I'm not buying it so I'm logging off and going to go dig up Adam, kick his dumper then have a raw turtle egg breakfast with pickled herring and lots of yellow creamery butter. Then I'm going to go kick Lucifer's dumper, pick up Eve and we're going to grab as many big red apples as we please, eat them, then jump in the rack for a week. After that I'm going to sit down and rewrite the whole mucking thing.

Note: Next session TBA.

LONG STORY MADE SHORT
Caroline Totten

Friday night. July 2006. The noisy restaurant on the beach was packed with locals and tourists, who were swilling beer and eating seafood while the huge TV screen flashed pictures of blood, guts, and gore. Hezbollah and the Israelis were duking it out with mortars. The TV sound was muted by the noise of the diners, who were venting. It was a conversational form born in tension and bathed in liquor. To the bourbon heads at the bar, Hezbollah, the army of god in black fatigues, was a bunch of arseholes; and their opponents, the Israeli troops, were dang Jews. By the time Don and his party of three were served dinner, the evening was in full swing.

Don, 53, half Cherokee Indian, half Irish, a flammable combo, glanced at the TV and complained that everything was out of control. He was bald and physically fit, except for old war wounds that flared painfully from time to time. His personal problem was that he could not find skilled carpenters to hire. The hassle was endless. The Mexicans were good workers, but most of them were illegal; and most of the local carpenters were in jail with a DUI.

Don lived on the Outer Banks, but was trying to build a house in the Smoky Mountains. He was having a devil of a time. He could not dig a well or put in a power line without bureaucratic paperwork weighted with fat fees. He needed a framing crew, but it could not be just anybody. The men had to know what they were doing. In a neighborly way, from his seat, he was asking around for house framers. He was offering to pay for gasoline and motel rooms until the house in Cherokee was complete.

When he turned back to his food, he grumbled that this house was going to cost him an arm and a leg. It irked him to pay $75 a week to fill the tank of his truck, and he was not the only one complaining.

At the wraparound mahogany bar, the talk was loud, bold, and participatory. Generally, the locals agreed with each other; the dissenters were into rapid eye movement and made comments like "Oh sheeit." The palaver went along some bumpy tracks such as: Oil companies were booming. They were raking in profits on the dog and pony show called supply and demand. Their cohorts, investment bankers, were buying up the rental property on the beach and sending dividends to their Arab investors. Everything was bull chips. Their grubby fishing village had morphed into a tourist attraction with bull chips–it was real estate parfume. Ha. Ha. It took a bull slinger to recognize bull chips. Essentially, ten minutes of hurricane would turn mansions into trash. Even so, real estate investment trusts were gambling on fair weather.

Don's son had no talent for construction or real estate, and he listened to all the talk in silence. Randy looked nothing like his father. He was overweight and had bushy, curly hair. He favored his mother–Don's ex-wife. Randy was eighteen and worked part-time as a trainee in another restaurant. He worked for minimum wage because he lacked experience. For months, he had been unemployed and living in his car in Frostburg, Maryland. When his father heard about it, he said, "Get your butt down here. You can live with Tara and me."

Tara, his second wife, forty going on twenty-eight, was a transplant, a Yankee from New England. She shifted her glance intermittently from the face of her husband to the bloody scene on the TV. She was a modern wife. She supported herself, but shared a home with her husband. They did not mix their assets because Don had trust issues. Divorce had nearly wiped him out financially. Worse than that, his ex-wife had driven him to drink, but eventually he dried out and went back to work. Now he did not touch a drop. He could not. It would kill him.

Don's guest was an old army buddy named James Stonerock Jackson, but called Jim. He was glancing at TV, dipping shrimp in horseradish sauce, and saying, "The Arabs have us by the tail. We buy the oil that supports them; now we gotta pay to fight them in Iraq and Stanisgan." Jim was a rough mountain boy. Never mind that he mispronounced Afghanistan. His specialty was making moonshine. He was passing through town and had stopped for a visit. He was drinking his own white lightning, which he carried in a flask in his vest pocket. Since Vietnam, he had lived in the mountains of West Virginia, hunting, fishing, and doing a little farming, stockpiling guns for when "the bastards (terrorists) take over Washington." He was convinced the country was going to hell, and he was ready to defend his plot of ground like a solid citizen.

The battle on the Israeli border, now flashing on TV, contrasted sharply with the partying in the restaurant. To Tara's mind, this was like the party that preceded a hurricane. Death and destruction needed the succor of spirits. Her sympathy was with the wounded and dying; and it was mixed with a kind of helpless anger. She could not do anything about the big picture, nor could she do much to fix her husband's problems. She sat and picked at her shrimp. She was tired, not festive.

Earlier in the day, she had done seven Swedish massages at the Manderling Spa. She was college educated and licensed by the state to pamper those tourists who could afford luxury. That morning she had tried to deposit her employment check in her checking account, but the bank would not accept it. Due to new security rules, McArnold, the simplified version of her name on the check, was not negotiable. It did not match the hyphenated version of Tara Smith-McArnold on the checking account. She had been depositing her employment check for years at the same bank and suddenly there was a problem, another hassle, one of many that had taken place since security measures on the beach had gone into paranoid mode.

When she stared at carnage displayed on TV, Jim tried to distract her. He remarked that he had his own missile system. He slept with a Smith&Wesson under his pillow and two rifles under his bed. "There's only one way to get peace," he said. "Tell Hezbollah they got eight hours. If the fighting doesn't stop, they get the big bomb." He dragged on his cigarette. "But we can't do that—cause it's imitating what we hate."

Tara sighed. "Here we are, stuffing our faces while other people are dying in Technicolor right before our eyes."

Young Randy, who had not said a word, finally offered a few. "Don't look."

"The way I see it," said Jim, "there are three kinds of people in the world. Those that are crazy; those that are half crazy; and those who don't know the difference."

Tara asked, "Which one are you?"

"I'm half crazy," he said with a loud belly laugh. He pushed back his chair. "I gotta get going. My daughter is expecting me. Figure I can make it to Mateo before midnight." He raised his hand in the gesture of a wave.

After he was gone, Don said, "He cleans up real good. Damn, he still has hair!"

Tara smiled. "Did he really save your life in Nam?"

"Yep. He's like a blood brother."

He turned to his son. "If we can get you in college, maybe you can skip the war."

"I have flat feet," said Randy as if that disqualified him for soldiering.

"Don't matter," said Don. "You got a trigger finger."

"Do you think Hezbollah will win?" asked Randy.

"Well, they're putting up a helluva fight, but win?" Don shrugged. "Nay."

Tara wiped a stinging wetness from her eyes. "There are no winners, Randy." She gripped her purse. "Let's go."

As they drove toward home, the sunset was like fire in the sky, and Tara was haunted by the vision of exploding bombs. Her spirit was struggling with some odd truth that was not completely clear. She felt feverish and grateful that they could go home, turn on the air-conditioner and sleep. Millions of people were unable to do that. Millions didn't want to do it, didn't want to put rage, hatred, or despair to rest.

She glanced across the sound and noticed the sea patrol monitoring the incoming boats. She was aware that they would have to stop at the checkpoint before they could get into their own neighborhood. It was as if the dark ghosts of the Middle East had invaded the beach. The simple act of going out to eat was like having dinner with death.

She gripped her husband's hand for comfort. Although he didn't say it, she knew why he was building a house in the mountains. Long ago, the Cherokee Indians had retreated to the mountains for safety. He had spent his childhood there, following his grandfather through the forest, learning survival skills. When the old man shot a deer, he honored its spirit. Expressing gratitude was clear and fundamental.

At the guardhouse, the officer recognized them and waved them through the gate. It was like drama, a subtle, somber drama. If the guard did not know you personally, you needed ID to enter the safe zone. It was ironic. The war had come to the beach in ways that were not so subtle. Tara thought: At the end of the day, home, behind the curtains, was where everyone was meant to be.

She turned on the light and climbed the steps. The house was built on stilts, but not impervious to flood or shifting sand. She walked softly, squeezed her fingers open, and shut like insect wings. She was okay. Of course, she was okay. Her role in the scheme of things was marginal, small as the white moth beating its wings against the light at the top of the stairs.

Medical Memoir

EXCERPT, *UNEXPECTED BLESSINGS IN THE MIDST OF MY PAIN*

Betty M. Smith

This final portion of the book gives insight about "Occipital Neuralgia" referred to as ON.

After being referred to many doctors and prescribed medication that did not work, my headaches became more intense. I was then not able to sleep and sleeping pills did not help. I was unable to find anyone that could help me. While surfing the internet for a doctor or clinic, My sister, Judy, from Chicago found Dr. Phyllis Zee, a Neurologist at Northwestern University. I was blessed to be able to get an appointment. She gave me a holistic plan that helped me sleep.

One cause of chronic headaches that is often overlooked is occipital neuralgia. Occipital Neuralgia is a type of headache that generally begins in the neck and then spreads up through the back of the head, causing throbbing, piercing pain. Often the scalp becomes tender, and sufferers may experience pain behind the eyes and become sensitive to light. Many people describe the pain as migraine-like, and the acute *symptoms* of Occipital Neuralgia can be at least as severe as those caused by a migraine.

Occipital Neuralgia can be caused by injury or irritation to the occipital nerves, which travel up from where the spine connects with the neck to the back of the head. Trauma to the back of the head or nerves compressed by swollen or tight neck muscles are the most common causes of this type of headache. Pressure on the occipital nerves can result in a worsening of symptoms, and physical tension often triggers an attack.

Upon returning to Canton from Chicago, I made an appointment with my primary care physician and discussed my visit to Chicago with Dr. Zee and Doctor H. She was very pleased with the results. We both agreed that I did not need to have any additional testing as recommended by Doctor H.

Every day the sun was out, I spent up to three hours outdoors. I started my exercise routine and scheduled an appointment with Dr. Wilcox for my "Cognitive Behavior Therapy." After two weeks of this routine, I began sleeping three to four hours a night. I would fax my sleep logs to Dr. Zee's office every ten days and within five days someone from her office would call and give me feedback. I was simply amazed at the support and care I received from Dr. Zee's office. The young lady who called was always so polite, kind and caring. With each log there would be different instructions to aid with my sleeping condition.

We have many great and caring doctors in this country and I'm sure their numbers exceed those who are not. It is my opinion that those who are not caring need to either live up to their oath of giving the best care possible to clients or find another profession. I feel they are giving the industry a bad reputation.

I continued Dr. Zee's treatment plan and in my sixth week, I began to sleep five and six hours each night. Never take sleep for granted. If you are able to sleep, you are BLESSED! I suggest that you not rely on sleeping pills, but try to find the cause for your inability to sleep. Are you stressed? Is it your diet? Do some research on your own. Get on the Internet and don't settle for one person's opinion. Most of all PRAY and ask God for guidance. Get in touch with your body. No one knows it better than God and you.

My sleeping definitely improved but my headaches continued. My pain was worse at night. The most severe pain was behind my left ear on the lesser occipital nerve. I would use hot and cold compresses, apply pressure with my fingers, and PRAY. After three or four hours, it would go away.

With Occipital Neuralgia you never know what to expect. Some days my head throbs, other days it feels as if it is in a pressure cooker, and yet on other days the pain is in the top of my head close to the area that is referred to as neuralgia and headache pain or sometimes the pain is in the front of my face like a sinus headache.

When the headaches appear at night, many times I'm unable to place my head on the pillow and am forced to sit up until the pain subsides. At times I try a rolled up large towel and place it under my neck. Another thing I try is a cervical pillow that can be placed in the freezer. I try one of these treatments until I find something that works.

I had the Fashion Show behind me but needed to fulfill two more commitments.

Maria, owner of Arcadia Grill in downtown Canton, is someone who genuinely cares about the needy and always tells me, "Betty, it's all about the babies. We must do whatever we can to take care of them." If you say, "My agency needs," before you finish the sentence she will say, "What can I do to help?" And, she helps everyone!

Every year Maria has "Christmas in July" and proceeds benefit agencies such as MDS, Domestic Violence Shelter, Community Services and the list is endless. She doesn't just do this in July, Maria has so many signs on her door for things she supports, you can't see inside her restaurant.

This year, because of my headaches, I was not able to stay for the entire event. Maria, who has breast cancer, seems to never miss a beat. She told me to go home and she would make sure our event was successful. What can you say about a person like Maria? She's definitely one of a kind!

My final commitment was to the Annual O'Jays Weekend that was scheduled for August 15-17 in Canton. I was responsible for the local PR. This is always a fun event and I enjoy working with the committee and interacting with the O'Jays.

The night before the major concert, that featured Frankie Beverly and Maze, The Whispers, and the O'Jays, I had a serious headache and was only able to sleep two hours. My videographer and I were scheduled to cover the entire event, which included setting up the stage, the "Love Train" ride with Eddie, capturing the crowd as they gathered for the event, and interviewing some of the committee members and guests.

My prayer was, "Dear Lord, please help me get through this last major event." I was full of coffee and re-energized from being in the sun that was truly bright and hot, 90 degrees. I had a wonderful time interacting with some awesome people, not only from Canton but from D.C., L.A., New York, Illinois and many other cities and states. We had a record crowd of 23,000 plus at Fawcett Stadium.

The next day I covered the O'Jays Parade on O'Jays Boulevard and the Family Reunion in Nimisilla Park. Monday morning we were at the historical William Powell Golf Course and that evening we met at the Pro Football Hall of Fame for the O'Jays Scholarship Banquet. I was blessed to interview HB Barnum a living legend in the music business, as a producer, songwriter, arranger and conductor for the biggest stars in history, including, Elvis, Sinatra, All the "Motown" stars, Lou Rawls etc. & musical director for Aretha Franklin for 35 years. Whew! I was definitely getting my three hours of sunshine and more than an hour of daily exercise. While I enjoyed each event, I was truly glad when this weekend was over. I had little or no sleep, but God was with me and helped me fulfill my commitment.

Now that the O'Jays weekend was over, I began to concentrate on my Retirement Party and the 10 Year Anniversary of Multi-Development Services of Stark County.

I was only going into the office one day a week and doing some work from home. Terrance was beginning to settle into the position and would call me when he had questions.

The MDS Board consists of some wonderful and dedicated folks. The President of MDS, Rod Meadows of Motter & Meadows Architects, a generous, kind and caring person, has been an avid supporter of MDS for the past five years. His concern for the agency and clients we serve is typical of his personality and character. Charleen Davidson, MDS Vice-President and one of the Assistant Vice-Presidents of Consumer Banking, has supported MDS since its inception. When I was unable to get a line of credit, it was Charleen, who at that time was with Unizan Bank, who stepped out and said, "Don't worry Betty, we'll give you a line of credit." And, Praise God they did.

Janet Haldeman, MDS Secretary and a resident of the Summit neighborhood, has been faithful for the past seven years. She loved working with young people making bears, quilts and other items. Her family has lived in the Summit neighborhood for more than 35 years.

Louise Bishop, MDS Treasurer whom I call my prayer warrior, is always available to help in the office or at events. Her prayers have definitely helped carry us through some very difficult times. She has been faithful for the past six years.

As long as my head was not hurting, I was still available for the monthly neighborhood clean up programs with the SNET II youth. I loved the interaction with the volunteers and neighbors.

September 26, 2009 is a day I shall always remember. This was the 10th Year Anniversary celebration for the Agency I founded, Multi-Development Services of Stark County, and my retirement.

The Board and Terrance planned a very memorable occasion that started when a limousine arrived to transport my husband and me to the event. Now that was special. The evening was filled with singing, testimonials, and a slide presentation highlighting many of the MDS programs.

The big surprise came when I was presented with a "Golden Dove Award." For the past ten years I would always present this award to others.

In my 12 years of living in Canton, I have been presented with numerous awards that include the Canton Negro Old Timers

Community Service Award, the Canton YWCA Women's Hall of Fame, Juneites Community Award, Deliverance Church Christian Hall of Fame, Beautiful People Award, Stark County Realtor's Association Community Award, Destiny Place Human Service Award and several others.

At the end of the celebration, I presented Terrance with a Bible and told him it was his "sword." I also told him that any and everything he needs is found in this wonderful book.

After the official ceremony, we had a lovely reception with good food and entertaining music provided by an MDS board member, Mia Macomson, referred to as Mia Morning.

During the month of October, I had two major attacks with pain behind my left ear. I remembered that I had a "pressure pump" and decided to use it. It definitely helped relieve the pain. For some reason, October 18th was the "best" pain-free day I had had in six months. I can't recall anything that I did that was different, but I gave God praise for the BLESSED day!

Janet Hawkins, who has been my herbalist for eight years, is dedicated and concerned about people's health issues. In 2003, when I had severe stomach pain and had an endoscopy and barium test that showed no problems, I tried all kinds of medication that did not help. Janet solved the problem with olive leaf drops and aloe vera! During one of my visits, I asked her if she knew anyone that administered colonics, the infusion of liquid into the colon through a tube in the rectum. I refer to a colonic as another form of taking an enema but with greater results! Big smile!

At that particular time she did not have a resource. Several years later, she introduced me to Linda Clifton, Founder of Crossroads Education and Wellness.

Linda and I became good friends. She is another person that cares and is concerned about people. Linda is constantly researching and looking for ways to better our health.

Twice a year Linda invites Dr. Dona Garofano, a Certified Nutritional Consultant, Certified Naturopathic Doctor in New Jersey, Certified Master Herbalist and a Licensed Health Officer in New Jersey to visit Crossroads and administer a Dried Blood Cell Analysis for registered clients. She also gives a power-point presentation to educate women about a healthier way of living with supplements.

In October I met with Dr. Garofano and was immediately impressed when I heard about her passion for helping women live a healthier lifestyle. She thoroughly explained to me that the DBA works by acquiring a sample of blood (with a small prick from the finger, which I voluntarily gave her). She then views the sample through a high-powered microscope to determine the imbalances present in the body created by the specific patterns the blood makes. These patterns, which set-up from the droplets, show areas of stress, acidity, toxicity, hormonal imbalance and the like.

She made it clear that the DBA is not a diagnosis, but a screening tool to analyze the present conditions of the body and help access nutritional needs of clients.

After my DBA, Dr. Garofano targeted areas in my body that were out of balance. She made recommendations of supplements that would bring my body back into balance. The body heals itself and needs nutrition in order for the healing to take place.

In our discussion she explained that the DBA is nothing new but was first introduced in Europe in 1920.

I informed her that I had been on Premarin for 28 years and had some doctors tell me to continue taking it and others said not to take it. One of Dr. Garofano's specialties is women's issues of hormonal, thyroid imbalances and adrenal stress that create symptoms such as depression, mood swings, weight gain, irritability and more. After she explained to me the dangers of Premarin, I decided to discontinue taking it. I now use Pure

Gest Progesterone crème and it is working fine.

Still in search for answers to many questions about my headaches and a possible cure for occipital neuralgia, Dr. Prowell told me I needed to find a Neuromuscular Therapist in my area since I was not able to come to Chicago as often as he needed to see me. I did an online search and, as God would have it, I found a gentleman named Michael Dallas Jones whose office was within 15 minutes from where I live. I clicked on his website at *www.fibromyalgiafullresolution.com*. Wow, what a story about this triathlete's life. I recommend that you read how he had to take charge of his body.

Michael treats all areas of the body including cranial sacral therapy and visceral (organ) massage. He has taken the St. Johns neuromuscular seminars. Additionally, he teaches those he treats how to do self-massage and shows them techniques to avoid overextending themselves.

Through email and phone Michael and I made an appointment for the two of us to meet. The following week, I met with Michael. We became instant friends!

He had some very informative videos for me to watch that were made in 1991 at the St. John Neuromuscular Pain Relief Institute in Largo, Florida. He also put me in touch with Dr. Leonard Knell, a retired Orthopedic Surgeon with 34 years of practice in Canton, OH, who validates Michael's treatment of Fibromyalgia and Occipital Neuralgia.

I discussed my book with Mike and told him I was wrapping up the final chapter and would like to meet with him for a statement on his practice. Mike also has a partner named Ross A. Carter. Mike and I set a meeting date for March 8. Dr. Knell would also attend this meeting

February 4, my husband and I traveled to Logansport, Indiana to the homegoing services for my oldest brother Freddie.

When I returned to Canton, I immediately made my water mixture and drank my usual gallon of water and began to make more time in my day to rest. I began to regularly juice carrots, celery, green peppers and apples as well as watch my intake of sugar and starch. I was feeling better.

I discussed this with Mike and he suggested until he has time to set up my treatment plan and get to the root cause of my headaches and intense pain to continue to only drink my bottled water.

While talking to God during one of my daily prayers, I so clearly heard Him tell me that this was my time to do things that I enjoy, to rest and focus on completing my book. I felt a peace and calmness that I had not felt in some time. It was wonderful feeling. I hated to move from the spot where I was praying wanting this feeling to last forever.

One month later, March 5, my husband and I once again traveled to Logansport but this time for a very happy occasion, the celebration of my Mother's 90th Birthday.

The night before the event we had a decorating party and a birthday celebration for my nephew Jaylon. I had serious pain behind my right ear but did not want the family to know I was suffering so I smiled and interacted with them as if everything was fine. That night I was only able to sleep three hours. The next morning, even though I was very tired, I did a 30 minute workout on the treadmill. I began to feel better.

My Mother's Birthday Party was a spectacular event that brought many local and out of state friends and relatives together. My oldest sister Melba did an outstanding job planning this party and her daughter Terri wowed us with her unique decorating skills. My other two sisters Wanda and Judy added their support to make this a wonderful event. Dwayne Lee from Chicago was the guest soloist. Family members included mother's children, grandchildren, great grandchildren and one of her two great-great grandchildren.

March 8 I met with Mike and Dr. Knell. We chatted, shared and laughed for 90 minutes. I feel so blessed to have met and be in the company of these two wonderful gentlemen. I set a date for both of them to appear on my local cable TV show. It is my desire that someone watching my show will be enlightened, helped and learn more about "occipital neuralgia." I am going to do more research and talk to others who are drinking the water to see what kind of results they are getting.

I know that in God's time, my headaches will be completely gone. He has the power to heal me or He can work through someone else. Either way, He is in control. Now, if I choose to continue working long hours, stay on the computer too long and other things that I know cause headaches, shame on me. God had to "break" me in order to "save" me! So, I am using what I have experienced to reach out and help others. I will do my best knowing that God will do the rest! By the way, my HDL is now 96 and my LDL is 199. This is without medication.

I continue to communicate with my friends on the MDJunction support line. These are truly a wonderful group of people with a sense of humor in spite of their pain. I told them that I do daily stretching exercises that help strengthen my neck and relieve my headache. Some of them asked that I share my tape, which I did. They are truly a BLESSING in the Midst of my Pain!

I pray my book has been a blessing. As Mike Jones, NMT, treats my Occipital Neuralgia, I will document every detail and pray. The outcome will be reported to you in my next book – one that reads "CURED!"

Contributors

A. D. ADAMS (TONY) is an engineer, patent holder, and drafts-man, who utilizes his spare time to write and create wood art. He has worked for Veyance Technologies, Goodyear Tire and Rubber, and Babcock and Wilcox. He authored the mystery "***Death on Lake Ice***" and the fantasy "***The Dragon Healer of Tone***". A. D. also edited the anthology "***Wordspinners of the Akron Manuscript Club***". For the 2009 Akron Children's Hospital Holiday Tree Festival, he created an all-wood tree, decorated with his lathe-turned ornaments, entitled "***A Woodmaker's Christmas***". A. D. designed the house where he resides with his wife Valentina.

DEANNA R. ADAMS is a Cleveland-area freelance writer, award-winning essayist, and author of three books. Her books include ***Rock 'n' Roll and the Cleveland Connection*** (Kent State University Press, 2002), ***Confessions of a Not-So-Good Catholic Girl*** (Infinity Publishing, 2008) and ***Cleveland's Rock and Roll Roots*** (Arcadia Publishing, 2010). Deanna is an instructor at Lakeland Community College, and The Lit (Cleveland's Literary Center), where she speaks and teaches on a number of writing topics. She is also director/coordinator of the Western Reserve Writers Conference at Lakeland Community College, and is founder of the Women Writers' Winter Retreat. Her web site is http://www.deannaadams.com.

BEN BARTMAN wrote his first poems in Texas where he grew up. He then moved to Berkeley (PhD, Chemistry), Boston (Postdoctoral studies), Philadelphia, and finally to Northeast Ohio. He spent his career leading industrial R&D. During that time he developed sev-eral interests and hobbies including building period furniture using old woodworking tools, biking, baking bread, and fishing. While he has written for himself for over 40 years, he has only written for others to read since January 2010. Ben's writings fall into three genres: love, nature, and giving voice to his search for his place in the world. The Cuyahoga Valley National Park is his inspiration for poetry, prose and life. The Russell Writers in Middletown, Connecticut gave birth to his joy for sharing his writings with others.

PEGGY BRUNYANSKY, former Fellow with the Wick Poetry Program at Kent, is a freelance writer and educator in North Canton, OH.

She has been active on the local poetry scene—writing, reading, publishing, workshopping and teaching—for more than thirty years. Her work has appeared in **The Huron Review**, **The Hiram Review**, and **Cantos**, among others.

GORDON BRYANT No biography available.

GREG BUTLER the father of two son's Zach-19 and Jacob-14. He has been married to wife Jan for 25+ years. He is the President and Owner of Alpha-Omega Assembly & Packaging Inc. In addition to being a member of the Massillon Rotary, he ran for Ohio State Central Committeeman this May. His hobbies include photography and writing.

"Prince Zachary" is a written story that originated as an oral bedtime story for his son Zach. When Zach was 5 he grew tired of **The Angry Ladybug, The Hungry Caterpillar**, etc. or maybe it was Greg who grew tired of reading them every night. One night Greg decided to make up a story and leave it as a cliff hanger for the next night. Thus the adventures of Price Zachary were born.

JUDI CHRISTY has been writing, in one form or another, since demanding a column (Judi's Prattle) in the *Elletian Star*, her high school paper, a publication she later edited. A journalism major (Kent State University), Judi's professional life has gained her professional kudos and publishing credits in scriptwriting, short stories, plays and the all-to-occasional corporate communiqués. An advanced degree in Curriculum and Instruction (The University of Akron), led her down the path of training and development at Goodyear and later, as a freelance designer and a writer for several years. She is also the founder of the Wednesday Writers Workshop. Currently, Judi is the Marketing Director for ArtsinStark, where she crafts promotional, fundraising and educational materials and organizes company hosted events. She also occasionally answers the phone, makes coffee and interjects witty commentary to conversations occurring amongst her co-workers. Judi Christy is married, has two children, and lives in Clinton, Ohio—with a dog named Reagan.

MARIE COX was born and raised in Ohio, but yearns for the sunshine and deserts of Arizona! Until her dream is achieved, she enjoys developing and teaching Composition and Literature courses at a local community college, where she holds the title of Associate Professor, English. A published poet and essayist, she now has an e-novel on Amazon's Kindle, **Murder by Deed**, which she is proud to say has already sold in the U.S., Canada, and the UK!

STEVE ENDRES' interest in birds started with a Boy Scout bird merit badge. His interest in photography started with a 35mm camera filming family vacation and occasional nature subjects. In 2007, at age seventy one, he combined birding and digital photography, and has been an avid bird photographer ever since. His bird images have won recognition in photo and art shows, and he has addressed bird groups. He continues to learn and take bird pictures.

LINDSEY FIGIEL is a twenty-five year old International Business major with a minor in Spanish at The University of Akron. She was born in Amersfoort, Netherlands and raised all over the world as a result of her father's being in the United States Air Force. She first learned about poetry and how to analyze it when she was in the fifth and sixth grade at Blair Elementary School in Spokane, Washington. During her high school years at Rocky River High School in Rocky River, Ohio, and Medina High School in Medina, Ohio, she started to write poetry as part of extra credit assignments for her English classes. She has continued her interest in poetry and wrote **Michael Dell** for her Honors Business Policy class at the University of Akron. **Michael Dell** is a poem about the leadership qualities of the founder and CEO, Michael Dell, of Dell Computers.

DANIEL GALLIK has multiple short stories and poems printed all over the internet, and in college journals. **Yes**, **The Hiram Poetry Review**, **Parabola**, **The Hawaii Review** and many other publications include his work. His first novel, **A Story Of Dumb Fate**, an insane story of a child with disabilities can be purchased at local bookstores and publishamerica.com, and for a reduced price from amazon.com Check out a summary of the book at www.danielgallik.com.

R. RAY GEHANI wrote his first three poems in 1971, and has published dozens of articles related to technological innovations since 1973 in leading professional journals. After studying and working in global tire-related industries for 12 years as a production engineer, new product developer, research engineer, project executive, and General Manager-Corporate Development, he switched careers to teaching business, and management of technology and innovation. He has a Bachelor's degree in chemical engineering, two master's degrees in textile technology and international business, two doctorate degrees in polymer science/engineering and business management, and a diploma in Japanese language.

In 1998, his seminal solo-authored book, **Management of Technology and Operations** was published by John Wiley & Sons, a leading publisher of business and engineering books. Almost 13 years later, it is still on sale on Amazon.com. In 2000, Dr. Gehani was selected as "20 Achievers to Watch in 2000" by Cleveland-based **Northern Ohio Live** magazine. He is a regular contributor, and an editor for **Lotus**, a Cleveland-based ethnic publication. He joined the Wednesday Writers Workshop in 2006 and has chaired the group since January 2008. In January 2010 he proposed the idea to compile and publish this anthology of poets and writers from the North-East Ohio. He is extremely delighted (with his co-editor Audrey Lavin) at the enthusiastic support by the leading authors in this community.

BARBARA M. HARKNESS retired from her profession as Professor of Anthropology at Kent State University, Kent OH, and turned to play writing. She has been equally successful in this second career. Her ten-minute plays *I Am a Ten-minute Play, The Beatification of Billy Goat Gruff,* and *The Distribution* have been performed in Seattle, Washington; Cincinnati, Ohio; and Cleveland, Ohio. In addition, her one act play At the Bridal Shop was part of the Cincinnati playwrights initiative and was competitive winner for staged readings in the New Voices contest.

CINDY HOLLIS No biography available.

BILL HOWLAND is a retired physician. He has published three books and 67 scientific articles. He enjoys writing short stories, small novels and poetry. Bill is a long-term actively attending member of the Wednesday Writers' Workshop.

NATHALIE KETTERER has scribbled all her life. Now she only writes the poems she feels compelled to write. Born in Wisconsin, she graduated from Marquette University there and then did a Master's at the State University of New York. Later she taught high school English off and on. More recently, she studied at Kent State with Poet Maggie Anderson and taught Basic Writing and Composition at University of Akron. For several years she has been a member of the Akron Manuscript Club, where members critique each other's work.

She hopes to publish a fourth collection of poems soon, having done two chapbooks and a full-length book. She is also working on a humorous (she hopes) tome, "***Empty Nesting 102***." When one of her sons died tragically five years ago, she memorialized his life in a memoir, "***Count Each Day***," published by Wheatmark. Individual poems of hers were originally published in various places, for example, "***Best of Ohio***," "***The Northern Reader***," "***Poetry***," and the "***Wisconsin Academy Review***." Some of these she read at Kent State, coffee houses, libraries, and bookstores.

Nathalie has lived in six different states, although she has visited all and beyond. Her present home is in Fairlawn, where she lives with her husband Ed. She has two grown kids, six grandkids, and three grand dogs.

LINDA TOLES LASLEY was born in Fredericksburg, Virginia. She and her husband moved to Ohio several years ago and currently reside in New Philadelphia, Ohio. She has enjoyed writing since her teen years. She writes short stories, poetry and children's stories. She is a member of the New Philadelphia Writer's Guild. She is now working on a collection of some of her short stories which she hopes to publish soon.

AUDREY LAVIN earned her Ph.D. in Literature at Case Western Reserve University (some years after her B.S. from Northwestern University). She has published two books on E. M. Forster and numerous essays, many in obscure literary journals. In addition to having been a Fulbright Professor two times in Spain, Dr. Lavin has been a Visiting Professor in 13 countries in Europe, Asia, Africa, and South America. She is also a founding member and past leader (five years) of the Wednesday Writers Workshop. As the author of *Eloquent Blood* and *Eloquent Corpse*, she is now looking for a publisher for her third murder mystery in the *Eloquent* series. She lives in Canton, Ohio, with her husband Carl and enjoys the comments she receives from her twice weekly *Whodunit?* blog at tr.im/whodunit

PHYLLIS LEE was born in Chicago and believes that if you walk down a red brick street at just the right time, it becomes a poem. Her work has appeared in **The Writer**, **Black River Review**, **North Star Two**, **She** (England), and numerous small press publications. She lives in Sebring, Ohio, with her husband, Dick.

JOSEPH McLAUGHLIN was an Associate Professor of English at Stark State College of Technology in Canton, Ohio, until his retirement in 2000. Now living in Dover, Ohio, he is a widely published writer whose poems, short stories, reviews, essays, travel articles and photographs have appeared in publications as diverse as **Mother Earth News**, **Stock Car Racing** and **Southern Poetry Review**.

KEVIN O'BRIEN was born in Canton, Ohio in 1957. He attended Our Lady of Peace, St. Thomas Aquinas high school, The Ohio State University and finally obtained his masters degree in pastoral counseling from Loyola University in Chicago. And while he has lived in different parts of the country and has done a myriad of different things, he finally has found his calling as a Funeral Celebrant—where he combines his writing abilities with his love of stories and ecumenical proclivity. His passions include writing haiku poetry, hiking in the woods, and sipping tea at Muggswigz Coffee and Tea shop in downtown Canton.

EUGENIA A. PARISH grew up in Canton, OH, but has mined her stories from all her travels. Her first short story was critiqued by her mother, who asked, "Does Alice in Wonderland really have to die?" From this she learned three things: the importance of considering your target audience; that grim is better than boring; and always listen to advice—not necessarily follow it, but always listen. Especially if it's your mother. Genie has had short stories published in several magazines as well as an essay in the **Journal of the Romance Writers of America**.

VALENTINA RANALDI-ADAMS attended the University of Akron, where she earned a Bachelor of Science Degree in Mathematics. She then worked for several years as a computer programmer for the Goodyear Tire and Rubber Company. Valentina has had haiku and poems published in *"Tributaries 9"*, *"Epitome"*, *"Paws and Whiskers"*, and the *"Yarrow Brook Literary Review"*. Her thoughtfully crafted poems speak in a voice that combines simplicity, eloquence, and humor. She also writes the newsletter for the Akron Manuscript Club, Ohio's oldest, continuously-meeting, writers' group. Valentina is married to author and wood artist **A. D. ADAMS** (a fellow-contributor).

SAM RETTMAN was born in Hof, Germany in 1946. He and his parents, both Holocaust survivors, immigrated to Canton, Ohio, in 1949. After attending Bowdoin College, Sam received a Masters Degree in Germanic Studies from Kent State University, He has also done graduate work in English literature. During his thirty-year career teaching high school English, German, Holocaust Studies, and Creative Writing, Sam also coached cross country and track. He has owned a white-water rafting company in Washington State, he has worked in home construction in Vermont and New Hampshire, and he has operated an animal rescue shelter. His three children live in Columbus, Los Angeles, and Denver. Currently, Sam loves to play music with his wife, Jennifer Maurer, a Northeast Ohio music legend.

G. L. ROCKEY went from the Carnegie Mellon Drama Department to earn a B.A. from Michigan State University and pursued a career in the television industry. From Providence to Phoenix and cities in between, he produced and directed a variety of television programs and managed TV station programming. While program manager at KTSP-TV in Phoenix, he represented NATPE (National Association of Television Program Executives) to Germany. He has a master's degree from Cleveland State University and taught a course there.

Rockey's works of fiction include novels: **The Journalist**; a political thriller; **Time & Chance**, mystery suspense; **Truths of the Heart**, romance suspense; and an anthology, **Bats in the Belfry, Bells in the Attic**. He has also written a nonfiction book, **From the Back of the House: Memories of a Steak House Clan**. Rockey currently writes article for **ScripType** magazines and is at work on a fourth novel. Keyword: G. L. Rockey; WEB SITE: www.glrockey.com.

INDRA SHAH (aka prof. I.K. Shah) was a professor of commerce and a professor of Law, in Ahmedabad, India. He emigrated to USA in 1971. His first book of poems, **Be Phool** was published in 1991. He has received a large number of awards for his professional legal and personal community service in Cleveland, Lake County, Ohio, and elsewhere. For example, he was appointed by the Supreme Court of Ohio as a member of the Ohio Bar examiners. He lives with his wife Minaxi, a system analyst. They have one son Sambhav, who practices medicine in Willoughby, Ohio.

BETTHY M. SMITH is an Indiana native and graduate of Northeastern Illinois University in Chicago. For 28 years she was employed by Catholic Charities of the Archdiocese of Chicago where she created many programs for youth and women in recovery. Betty began her television career in Chicago where she hosted a fitness and talk show. She was an aerobics instructor and trainer in her "Stretchnastics" fitness studio. In 1998 Betty married Rev Mark M. Smith and moved to Canton. In 1999 she founded Multi-Development Services of Stark County, a not-for-profit social service agency. She also created Canton Idol, Downtown NU-Zone Festivals, Golden Dove Awards and Gospel Joins Symphony. She retired as Executive Director in September, 2009.

For the past ten years, she has hosted "On Track with Betty Mac", Channel 11, Canton City Schools TV. In 2008 and 2009 she was the Chairman of the Pro Football Hall of Fame Enshrinement Festival's Fashion Show; she serves on the Board of Directors for Canton Symphony Orchestra; a graduate of the 19th class of Leadership Stark County and serves on the Professional Advisory Committee for Malone University. In her 12 years in Canton she has served on numerous committees and boards and received 7 community awards. She enjoys walking and music. Her husband is Rev. Mark M. Smith, Pastor, Jesus Speaks Christian Center.

JOE TORMA is Professor of Theology at Walsh University, Ohio. He has a B.A. degree from Gannon College, M.A. degree from the University of Detroit, and Ph.D. from the University of Ottawa. His specialties include: Church in the Modern World, Social Work, Community Service, the Church and Social Action, Catholic Social Ministry. He teaches courses including Principles of Justice and Peace, Social Ministry.

CAROLINE TOTTEN is a former newspaper reporter who invents a mosaic of fiction and reality in her many published stories. Recently, her story **Down and Dirty** appeared in the anthology **Dead Worlds, Undead Stories**, Volume 4. **An Apocalyptic story, Life Among the Ruins**, is slated for the October 2010 Bellfire Press anthology. One of her Internet publication, **By the Sea, By the Sea**, (Innsmouth Free Press) appeared in 2009, and **The Politics of Famine**, (2009 Stottsberry Award) has been reprinted at CantonWritersGuild.org. She is a native of Canton and she formerly taught Novel and Short Story Writing at Kent Stark Campus.

CAROLYN WELDON was born at the end of the Great Depression and is still here. Her family came to Akron, Ohio, from rural Pennsylvania when she was three. A couple of years later, her father left to serve in the U.S. Navy/South Pacific two days before Christmas. Her family was lucky: he came back. Carolyn attended Akron Public Schools and earned her Bachelor of Science in Elementary Education from The University of Akron.

Carolyn's interests include baseball, music, writing, and T'ai Chi. Her childhood hero was Joe DiMaggio. At the age of five Carolyn had the ability to pick out songs by ear on the piano. Her parents bought her a secondhand piano and sent her to the neighborhood piano teacher. Music became a part of her life and eventually led her to a marriage with a musician for 33 years. She is a mother of two sons.

Carolyn began writing in the sixth grade at the prompting of her teacher.

Her poetic inspiration came in her mid-teen years while reading "**Death of the Ball Turret Gunner**", by Randall Jarrell. Her love of poetry continued in college where she studied with Elton Glaser, who continues to be a mentor and inspiration. Carolyn has also studied with Maggie Anderson, and is a long-time member of the Akron Manuscript Club.

Her poetic inspiration comes from her travels in the Southwest United States and her love of animals. Currently, Carolyn is writing a compilation of poems on dogs, cats, and an occasional reptile or rodent. The ideas for these poems come from her long days as a caretaker of the beloved pets of neighbors and friends. Her poems have been published in state and national award-winning poetry collections.

THERESA WOODS is a bookkeeper by trade and a poet/artist by heart. An active member of the Canton Poetry Society, she enjoys doing poetry readings around her hometown, Canton, Ohio. Her work, including "*September Shoe Time*," which appears here, has won awards in Ohio Poetry Day contests.